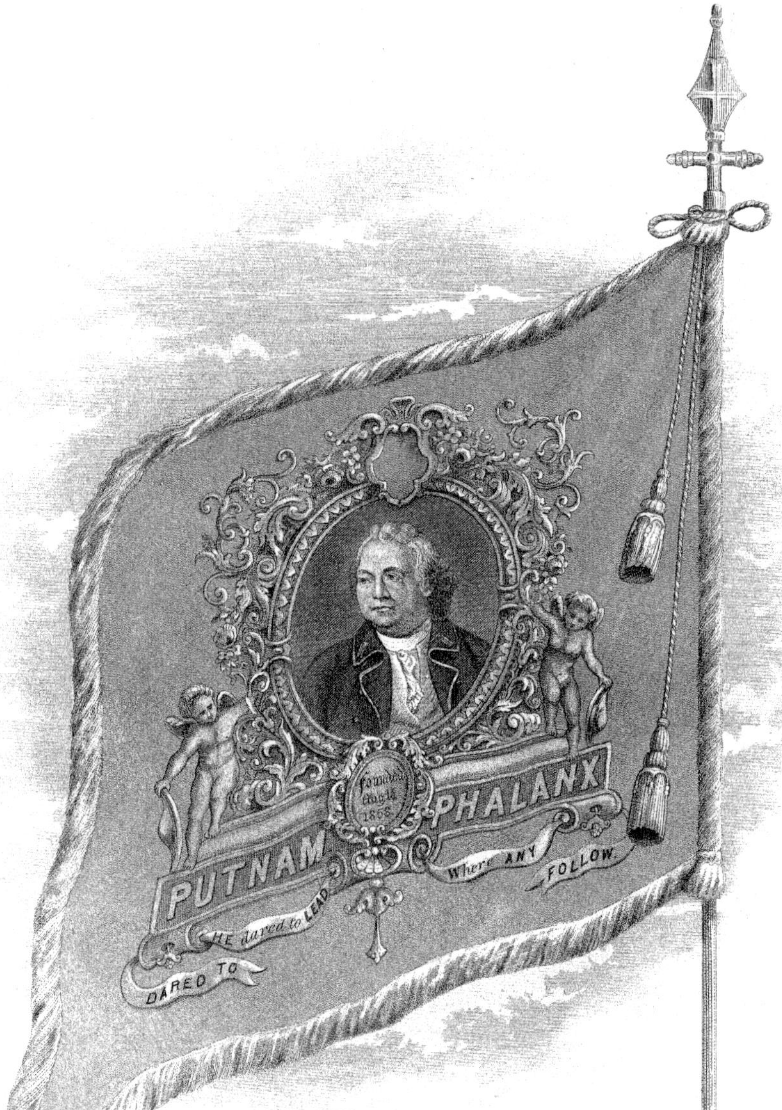

Engraved by J. C. Buttre, New York.

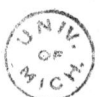

EXCURSION

OF THE

PUTNAM PHALANX

TO

BOSTON, CHARLESTOWN AND PROVIDENCE,

OCTOBER 4TH, 5TH, 6TH AND 7TH,

IN THE YEAR OF OUR LORD 1859.

HARTFORD, CONN:
PUBLISHED BY THE PHALANX.
1859.

PRINTED AT HARTFORD, CONN.,
BY CASE, LOCKWOOD & CO.

PREFATORY.

THE Putnam Phalanx, defirous of putting in permanent form a Complete Record of their recent Excurfion to Bofton, Charleftown and Providence, confided the tafk of its preparation for publication to one who is not a member of their Organization. With him the labor has been one of careful collation and of furnifhing fuch thread of narrative as was neceffary to connect the various Addreffes and more important Incidents of the Excurfion, which were extenfively reported in the Journals of the day. In a publication emanating from the Phalanx, it has feemed proper to avoid particular comment upon the performances of individuals, and generally to omit the enthufiaftic encomiums of the prefs which were lavifhed upon the prominent members of the Organization. It is but fimply juft that the entire credit of thefe journeyings, and of the brilliant feries of receptions, fhould be attributed to the Battalion as a body — not forgetting thofe courteous and hofpitable friends in the Cities vifited, whofe unwearied efforts and attentions contributed fo largely to the fuccefs, as well as pleafure of the Excurfion.

Care has been taken to obtain revifed copies of the Addreffes from the various Speakers. The thanks of the Putnam Phalanx are refpectfully and cordially tendered to Mrs. L. H. Sigourney, for the beautiful poem on *General Putnam*, and to George H. Clark, Efq., for the exquifite lines upon the affecting incident at Moofup — both of which were kindly furnifhed exprefsly for this publication.

R.

Hartford, November, 1859.

GENERAL PUTNAM.

REAT Soul, and brave, 'tis good to think of thee,
And with a filial reverence raife the veil
From patriot valor, that ne'er fought of Fame
Her clarion-payment.

   See we not again,
The unfinifhed furrow, the forfaken home,
The flying fteed, urg'd by thy fleeplefs heart
That throbb'd indignant o'er a fmother'd found,—
The cry of *Lexington?*

   That echoed cry
Rous'd a young nation from its lingering fleep
To rufh againft the force of tyrant power,
Time-confecrated, and with fling and ftone
Defy the giant.

   Bunker Hill records
Thy ftern o'ermaftery of the battle-ftorm,
The deep memorial of thy dauntlefs deeds
That bore the fpirit of a trampled land,
Through this red preface of her liberty.

Hark!—from the heaving of yon burial fods
Where fleep our Country's champions, comes a voice
Demanding for thy name its juft reward
Too long withheld.—Of Hiftory it demands
That lingering truth fhould light her lettered fcroll,
And fummons tardy man to fet thy fame
In fculptured marble, that recording ftars
May read it clearly from their filver thrones,
And lifping children from its tablet learn
What patriot virtue means.

         L. H. S.

EXCURSION.

AT a Special Meeting of the Putnam Phalanx, held at their Armory on the evening of September 18th, it was unanimoufly refolved that the Phalanx as a body fhould make a Pilgrimage to Bunker Hill, and a brief vifit to Bofton, Charleftown and Providence. *Quarter-Master* Strong proceeded to thofe places to make the neceffary arrangements, and at a fubfequent meeting, the 4th, 5th, 6th and 7th days of October were felected as the time for the propofed Excurfion. After due confideration, the Phalanx decided to invite but two perfons to accompany them as Guefts of the Battalion, viz: his Excellency Governor Buckingham, and ex-Governor Seymour, of Connecticut. To the great regret of the Organization, the Secretary received the following letters, refpectfully declining the invitation:

FROM GOVERNOR BUCKINGHAM.

STATE OF CONNECTICUT, }
Executive Department. }
Norwich, September 30th, 1859.

J. M. SEXTON, ESQ.,
Sec. Putnam Phalanx,

Dear Sir: I have the pleafure of acknowledging your favor of the 28th inft., conveying the invitation of the Putnam Phalanx to be their gueft during an Excurfion to Bofton and Providence, and beg you to affure that diftinguifhed body that it would give me great pleafure to be with them a portion of the time; but an engagement in Philadelphia on the 4th, 5th and 6th of Oct. muft deprive me of fuch high gratification. You will alfo affure them that I highly appreciate the honor of fuch an invitation and that their fentiments of regard as expreffed by you are cordially reciprocated.

I am with great refpect your obedient fervant,

WM. A. BUCKINGHAM.

FROM EX–GOV. SEYMOUR.

Hartford, Oct. 3d, 1859.

Dear Sir: I am in the receipt of your efteemed favor of the 28th *ult.*, inviting me, in behalf of the Putnam Phalanx, to become their gueft on their contemplated Excurfion to Bunker Hill. In reply, I regret to ftate that circumftances will prevent me from having that honor. Several engagements of an unavoidable kind requiring my prefence in Hartford, or New York, during the time the Phalanx will neceffarily occupy on their way to and from Bofton, Bunker Hill, and the other places they will vifit, forbid the pleafure of accepting their friendly invitation.

The unanimous vote of the Phalanx making me their gueft for the coming Excurfion, adds another to the deep obligations I am under to your Honorable Affociation, and calls for a renewal of my grateful acknowledgments, which, I beg you will have the goodnefs of prefenting to the Battalion, in my behalf.

Hoping the moft favorable circumftances will attend your footfteps to the *Holy places,* and bring you all fafely back to us, where a hearty welcome will await you, I have the honor to be your faithful fellow-citizen and very obedient fervant,

THO. H. SEYMOUR.

HORACE GOODWIN, ESQ.,
Major Com't Putnam Phalanx.

THE DEPARTURE.

On the morning of Tuefday, October 4th, the Phalanx affembled in full force and uniform at their Armory, and fhortly after eleven o'clock, marched to the Station, under command of *Major Com't* Goodwin, and accompanied by their Drum Band. The following is the Mufter-Roll of the Battalion:

OFFICERS OF THE PUTNAM PHALANX.

HORACE GOODWIN, *Major Commandant.*

Gen. Lloyd E. Baldwin acting *Adjutant* for the Excurfion, by appointment of the *Major Commandant.*

STAFF OFFICERS.

Jofeph D. Williams, *Adjutant;* Eugene B. Strong, *Quarter-Master;* James B. Crofby, *Pay-Master;* Benning Mann, *Commiffary;* Henry C. Deming, *Asfiftant Commiffary;* I. W. Stuart, *Judge Advocate;* Afher Moore, *Chaplain;* Thomas Miner, *Surgeon;* D. P. Francis, *Affiftant Surgeon;* William Ifham, *Sergeant-Major;* Charles T. Martin, *Quarter-Master Sergeant;* Julius M. Sexton, *Secretary.*

OFFICERS OF FIRST COMPANY.

Allyn S. Stillman, *Captain;* James B. Shultas, 1*st Lieut.;* T. M. Allyn, 2*d Lieut.;* Allyn Goodwin, *Enfign;* Geo. W. Hayden, 1*st Serg't;* C. C. Burt, 2*d Serg't;* S. E. Marfh, 3*d Serg't;* Samuel Alexander, 4*th Serg't;* H. S. Larkum, 1*st Corp'l;* Edmund Hurlburt, 2*d Corp'l;* H. L. Brown, 3*d Corp'l;* L. M. Bacon, 4*th Corp'l.*

OFFICERS OF SECOND COMPANY.

Alexander M. Gordon, *Captain;* O. D. Seymour, 1*st Lieut.;* J. H. Afhmead, 2*d Lieut.;* Wm. J. Denflow, *Enfign;* Edward Norton, 1*st Serg't;* J. L. Wilder, 2*d Serg't;* J. M. Greenleaf, 3*d Serg't;* N. G. Hinckley, 4*th Serg't;* J. H. Williams, 1*st Corp'l;* T. C. Allyn, 2*d Corp'l;* F. A. Cary, 3*d Corp'l;* John T. Fenn, 4*th Corp'l.*

Otis Smith, *Standard Bearer.*
Color Guard.—A. W. Birge, Hez. Huntington, H. L. Miller, Chas. B. Smith, Col. Sam'l Colt, E. D. Tiffany, C. C. Stetſon.

Privates.

N. R. Alford, J. H. Auſtin, Geo. Burnham, Albert Barrows, Wm. H. Bradley, H. B. Beach, Henry Bolles, Horace Billings, J. C. Bartlett, A. W. Birge, Hiram Biſſell, John H. Brainard, Leverett Brainard, Lloyd E. Baldwin, E. J. Baſſett, Wm. N. Bowers, L. M. Beaumont, C. M. Bidwell, W. F. J. Boardman, S. S. Bolles, A. L. Cooley, A. E. Clapp, E. W. Clark, D. C. Corniſh, Sam'l Colt, A. Chicheſter, Julius Catlin, Caleb Clapp, W. P. Chamberlin, W. R. Chapman, Moſes Cook, John L. Cook, A. L. Cady, S. D. Crane, H. W. Conklin, Wm. M. Charter, Jos. Davis, Wm. H. Dobie, H. D. Downing, O. M. Drake, Gaylord Dowd, Wm. J. Denſlow, Jr., A. D. Euſon, Oliver Ellſworth, Frederick Ellſworth, Irad Edwards, J. M. Farnham, Wm. Frazier, John I. Farwell, Walter Fox, Amos Fowler, E. G. Francis, J. B. Green, J. T. Gorton, John M. Groſs, Edward Goodman, C. H. Goodman, F. L. Gleaſon, A. C. Griſwold, Francis Gowdey, W. R. Hopkins, W. C. Higley, W. H. Henderſon, Sam'l Hubbard, D. L. Hayden, M. O. Hills, Cheſter Hebard, Hezekiah Huntington, John S. Huffey, H. D. Haſtings, E. P. Harrington, H. P. Hubbard, H. Sidney Hayden, Thos. R. Haſkell, A. P. Jordan, Pliny Jewell, Jr., E. N. Kellogg, Hawley Kellogg, Henry Kennedy, S. B. Kendall, F. T. Lucas, W. B. Leonard, Jas. Loomis, 2d., Marinus Lord, James Lockwood, Geo. Marſh, J. H. Moſt, Rob't McCriſtie, H. L. Miller, D. A. Mills, Jas. T. Pratt, Dan'l B. Phelps, Chas. Parſons, Guy R. Phelps, R. R. Phelps, L. F. Pariſh, Jos. Pratt, Oliver Pariſh, A. P. Pitkin, L. K. Parſons, Dan'l Potter, R. P. Pratt, Daniel Phillips, Rawſon Read, Horatio Root, E. M. Roberts, Wm. S. Ramſey, H. B. Rhodes, J. M. Riggs, J. T. Roberts, W. K. Ranney, Gurdon Robbins, Jr., John G. Root, Timothy Sheldon, C. C. Stetſon, J. H. Sharp, Otis Smith, Francis Swan, Maſon Smith, Chas. B. Smith, Geo. G. Sill, Milo Shepardſon, Eliſha Smith, Wm. H. Seymour, Stiles D. Sperry, James Spencer, J. K. Southmayd, Alvin Squires, William Tuller, E. B. Thomas, E. D. Tiffany, S. S. Thompſon, Geo. C. Waſhburn, Geo. L. Way, J. W. Weeks, R. R. White, V. W. Whiting, Horace Waters, Everett Wilcox, W. F.

Whittlefey, H. W. Wright, J. K. Wheeler, Wm. J. Whipple, S. A. White, Wm. Wright, C. C. Waite, H. L. Whiting.

Honorary Members.

A. E. Burr, Thos. Belknap, F. A. Brown, J. Watfon Beach, Geo. Brinley, Putnam Brinley, E. H. Brinley, Newton Carter, Geo. H. Clark, Ezra Clark, Jr., H. K. Carter, J. W. Danforth, Lorenzo Daniels, S. A. Enfign, Wm. P. Fay, Horace Freeman, Jas. M. Goodwin, E. T. Goodrich, Wm. Jas. Hamerfley, Chas. I. Hills, W. M. B. Hartley, Henry Keeney, W. H. Kelfey, E. T. Lobdell, Geo. S. Lincoln, Charles Lincoln, Uriah Litchfield, J. M. B. McNary, Geo. W. Moore, C. H. Northam, Solomon Porter, Timothy Porter, L. F. Robinfon, L. Rowell, Benj. D. Rockwell, D. A. Rood, Burrall Sage, Wm. B. Smith, Sam'l G. Savage, Thos. H. Seymour, Sam'l L. Talcott, E. B. Watkinfon, Sam'l Woodruff, A. A. Williams, E. W. Williams, Henry Williams, Wm. L. Wood.

Volunteers for the Excursion.

W. S. Roberts, *ex-Capt. Hartford Light Guard;* Geo. S. Burnham, *Col. 1st Reg. Conn. Militia; ex-Major* A. E. Birge; Geo. A. Burnham, *ex-Capt. Seymour Light Artillery;* Julius L. Rathbun; H. D. Tarbell; G. Stillman; A. H. Benjamin; H. Enfworth, *Adjutant 1st Reg. Conn. Militia;* F. P. Lepard.

Drum Band.

H. T. Chapin, Nathan L. Robinfon, J. M. Perry, Almon H. Bruce, S. G. Wilcox, D. H. Wilcox, L. C. Miner, Rob't Mofeley, Thos. M. Perkins, James Stone.

Camp Attendants.

Henry Hector, J. F. Rodney, J. L. Cambridge.

The Phalanx never appeared in better drill and difcipline, nor attracted more attention at any of their previous parades than on their march to the Station. At this point, a large Crowd was affembled to witnefs their departure. Three of the paffenger and two of the baggage cars of the long train were fpecially appropriated to the Battalion and were completely filled. The train ftarted at the regular hour, and as the cars left the Station, cheer after cheer rofe from the Crowd of friends whofe warmeft wifhes for the complete fuccefs of the Excurfion and fafe return of the Battalion accompanied them. At Windfor Locks, a gun faluted the paffing train; at Springfield, the Depot was thronged with people anxious to fee the Phalanx; at Worcefter, and all along the route at every Station, the Phalanx was greeted with throngs of appreciative fpectators — happy auguries of the Reception that awaited them at Bofton.

THE ARRIVAL AT BOSTON.

The train by which the Phalanx was to arrive was due at the Worcefter Depot at half paft four o'clock, and at that hour the ftation and adjoining ftreets were thronged with people. The train, however, was fo heavily loaded that it did not arrive till twelve minutes paft five. The rear cars which contained the Battalion were immediately furrounded by an enthufiaftic crowd, anxious to catch the firft fight of the Corps which came out from the Depot on Kneeland ftreet, amid the booming of cannon fired by the Light Artillery Company, *Capt.* O. F. Nims, and marched from there in fingle file to Lincoln ftreet, on the fouth fide of Kneeland, where they formed as a Battalion, and marched to Beach ftreet, in front of the United States Hotel, where they were greeted with continuous cheers, and where the Mayor and numerous Municipal officers and citizens were in waiting to tender a formal Reception and Welcome. Much credit is due to the admirable and efficient arrangements of the Bofton Police, by means of which the fpace in front of the Hotel was kept open for the evolutions of the Phalanx. When the Battalion was drawn up in line, Mayor Lincoln, accompanied by the City Officers and others, appeared upon the fteps of the Hotel and was introduced to the Corps by Oliver Ellfworth, Efq.,—formerly of Hartford and now a refident of Bofton—a member of the Phalanx. The Mayor was received with a falute by the Drum Band—the Battalion prefenting arms; after which his Honor welcomed the Putnam Phalanx to Bofton in the following addrefs:

Mayor Lincoln's Welcome.

Mr. Commander:—It affords me great fatisfaction to welcome you and the Battalion under your command to the City of Bofton. Our citizens are often gratified with the vifits of military friends from other Cities or States of the Union, but it is many years fince we were honored by the prefence of a Corps from the good State of Connecticut or the City of Hartford. I welcome you in my official capacity as Mayor of the City, and on one account I wifh we were affembled at our City Hall, for I could point you to a fpot which has affociations as dear to you, Natives of Connecticut, as it is to us, Sons of Maffachufetts. From the windows of our City Hall we look into the moft ancient of our burial places; within its facred enclofure is a tomb where reft the remains of a Father and Son. The Father was the firft Governor of Maffachufetts Bay, the fon held a fimilar pofition in your own infant Colony. While we boaft with pride of the virtues and fervices of the elder Winthrop, you render a fimilar tribute to the younger. Together their afhes are mingled in the common duft.

The union and community of intereft, thus fymbolized in our early Chief Magiftrates, has always exifted between the people of our refpective Commonwealths. Together they ftood, fhoulder to fhoulder, when we were feeble Colonies, in the ftruggles with the Indian Tribes in the Old French War, and in the glorious Revolutionary conteft, which achieved the Independence of the Nation.

You appear to us to-day, not only as Sons of Connecticut, but in the military coftume of the Revolutionary era. In your drefs and martial bearing, you would remind us of the peerlefs Wafhington and the Fathers of the Republic. You recall to our memories the Patriots who defended their country in the time of peril, and left us the pricelefs inheritance which we now enjoy.

To defignate your Corps, you have taken the name and infcribed on your banner that noble Revolutionary Hero, who, like the Roman Cincinnatus, left his plow in the field to haften to the relief of his ftruggling Countrymen. With the brave, he was the braveft, for it was faid of Putnam that "he dared to lead where any dared to follow."

Reprefenting as you do, gentlemen, by your peculiar Organization, the Revolutionary period, we bid you welcome to the fcenes of its earlieft conflicts. The part the old Town of Bofton took in that Conteft makes one of the moft important pages in its Hiftory. You come as Pilgrims to its Holy Shrines; may you find that the Defcendants are worthy of their Sires, and that the Principles of Liberty here promulgated by the Fathers, are ftill held dear by their Sons.

Your Charter Oak has fallen to the ground. A fimilar fate may await our Faneuil Hall, and it may crumble to the earth; but the principles which gave them their glory fhall never die, but fhall continue unimpaired through the march of Ages and the progrefs of Time.

Again I unite with the Citizens of Bofton here affembled, and give you a moft cordial greeting and welcome.

Major Goodwin then introduced *Judge Advocate* Stuart, who responded to the Mayor's welcome in the following words:

Response of Judge Advocate Stuart.

Your Honor Mayor Lincoln:—For the prefent manifeftation of your courtefy, for the kind and eloquent words of welcome with which you, Sir, have greeted the Putnam Phalanx, they return you their heartfelt thanks. We come hither, organized, as your Honor perceives, as a peculiar Corps, to feek in your City, and in its precincts, peculiar enjoyment. We come as a Battalion organized, not only for the purpofe of commemorating that early Paft to which you have so eloquently referred, but also, and more especially, to aid in invigorating the glorious memories of that Revolution in which Boston played so conspicuous and leading a part—to which not only your City, but Massachusetts all, Connecticut, New England all, more than any other portion of our common Country, devoted, without stint, their blood and their treasure—and which, through each one of its magnificent results, comes knocking daily for gratitude at the heart of every inhabitant of this Union.

We seek, Sir, the shrines of an Otis, a Thacher, a Hancock, a Quincy, an Adams, a Warren, a Prescott,—of all those noble Patriots and gallant men who here led the van of opposition to Great Britain, when that mighty Monarchy commenced her career of aggression upon her American Colonies, and began to launch against them the thunderbolts of war.

Not, Sir, that we forget that mighty Past which preceded the American Revolution, to which you have so impressively referred. We do not. We honor and revere the upright and accomplished Governor John Winthrop, the Father of the Massachusetts Colony, as he is justly termed, and we lay special claim to the renown of John Winthrop, his son, and of John Fitz Winthrop, his grandson, Governors both of them, as they were, of old Connecticut.

But the Revolutionary Past of Boston—that is what now more immediately concerns our Phalanx. The City over which you preside, Sir—we know it—it is familiar truth, the world knows it by heart—*was* emphatically the cradle of American Liberty. Here, we are aware, glowed the first watchfires, and blazed from your hills the first beacon lights that summoned America to arms. Here, in venerable Faneuil Hall and in your old State House were poured forth the first indignant strains of eloquence and fiery resolves, which, after the Peace of Paris, greeted with grave scorn and stern menaces of resistance the opening tyranny of our Motherland. And here, too, within hail of your memorable City—at Lexington, at Concord, at Bunker Hill—was shed the earliest blood of the Revolution—seed-blood, as it proved to be, of the most gigantic, perilous, and triumphant struggle for Liberty that the World has ever seen.

We of this Phalanx, Sir, therefore feel—under the view I now suggest—that we stand in this City upon consecrated ground—ground consecrated by the love and labors not only of those noble Patriots to whom I have already referred, but also of many more, who here led that Revolution which it is our fpecial object to commemorate. We would look, therefore, upon the localities diftinguifhed by their zeal and fervices. We would gaze upon the fpot where flood that memorable tree whofe Genius, though invifible, is faid to have always found pens, and ink, and paper, and a hoft of witneffes, for every patriotic compact of your Bofton Sons of Liberty.

We would look, yet once again, upon your world-renowned Cradle of Liberty — old Faneuil Hall. We would gaze upon the fpot where the daring Patriots of Bofton gave ocean-burial to the peftilential teas. And, efpecially, we would make our pilgrimage to Bunker Hill — from that hallowed fpot to catch frefh infpiration for our Patriotifm, and there to renew vows of devotion to our beloved Country.

Thefe, Sir, are the main purpofes of our vifit to Bofton — thefe, and the interchange of pleafant converfation and courtefies with any who may defire to hold communion with us.

To the thoufand ftirring memories which meet and greet us here in this City, we of this Phalanx — with becoming modefty I fay it — can add a rich Revolutionary ftore of our own; for we bring with us from old Connecticut the memories of a Trumbull — that immortal "Rebel" Governor of his day, and of a Sherman, an Ellfworth, a Williams, a Dyer — of that gallant Putnam, to whom your Honor has fo eloquently referred — of a Hale, a Knowlton, a Spencer, a Douglafs, and of thirty-one thoufand nine hundred and thirty-one of her Sons, whom, in the times that tried men's fouls, Connecticut devoted to the battle-fields of their Country.

That we may pleafantly mingle thefe our Revolutionary affociations with thofe of hiftoric Bofton, and of the old Bay State, is, Sir, the hearty hope of the Putnam Phalanx.

Mr. Stuart's fpeech was frequently interrupted with hearty outburfts of applaufe, and at the clofe the Speaker and the Phalanx were loudly cheered.

The line was then re-formed, and the Battalion marched to the Armory of the Second Battalion of Infantry, in Boylfton Hall, where they depofited their guns and partook of the well known hofpitality of the Infantry. *Major* C. O. Rogers briefly welcomed the Phalanx to the City.

The Second Battalion had ornamented the front of their Armory with fome fplendid decorations. In front was an illuminated portrait of Wafhington, over which was the infcription "1776—Union—1859." Below was the name "Wafhington," between two ftars. Several lines were ftretched acrofs Wafhington ftreet, on which were fufpended flags, and ftreamers, and from a point near the building two lines depended, with Chinefe lanterns attached. (Thefe formed a fplendid illumination in the evening.) After fome time fpent in pleafant intercourfe and mutual introductions, the Phalanx returned to their Quarters at the United States Hotel, partook of fupper and devoted the evening to receiving their friends and entertaining new acquaintances. A portion of the Phalanx, by invitation of *Commander* Rogers, vifited the Armory of the Second Battalion of Infantry again in the evening. On their arrival the Drill-Mafter of the Battalion being prefent, the Infantry Officers propofed to gratify their Guefts by an exhibition of the Zouave drill. In ten minutes time, about thirty Infantrymen were prefent in uniform and went through with the drill with admirable precifion and rapidity of movement. Not fatiffied with this courtefy, the Officers infifted upon a vifit to the "Captain's Office" adjoining the Armory. Here there was a renewal of the hofpitalities for which the Infantry are fo famous. *Major* Rogers again expreffed his gratification at the vifit of the Phalanx. *Capt.* Gordon announced that the command of the members of the Second Company devolved *pro tempore* upon *Second Lieutenant* Afhmead, who accordingly refponded briefly. He thanked the Officers of the Second Infantry for this unexpected and additional pleafure of the evening. The members of the Phalanx prefent, he remarked, were delighted with the beautiful drill they had juft witneffed and warmly appreciated the courtefies of their Hofts, who had been unremitting in their attentions to the Phalanx during their vifit. After an hour or more of focial intercourfe and an examination of the pictures and relics in this beautiful Armory, the vifitors returned to their Head-Quarters for the night.

THE VISIT TO CHARLESTOWN AND BUNKER HILL.

Shortly after nine o'clock on Wednefday morning, the Charleftown City Guards, numbering 54 guns, accompanied by the Brigade Band, left their Armory and marched to the Tremont ftreet Mall of the Common, where a halt was made. A committee was then fent to the Armory of the Second Battalion, where the Phalanx were under arms, and efcorted them to the Common, where they were received by the Guards with the cuftomary military falutes. Immediately after, the line of march was taken up, and the Guards with their guefts proceeded through Tremont, Court, Green and Caufeway ftreets to Charleftown. An open carriage drawn by a beautiful fpan of grey horfes contained the *Commiffary*, *Affiftant Commiffary* and *Judge Advocate*, and after the battalion had proceeded fome diftance the *Major Commandant* alfo took a feat in it, but refumed his command at Charleftown. The entire line of march from Bofton to the Monument grounds was thronged on both fides with fpectators, every window feemed filled with fmiling faces of fair ones who waved their welcomes, and as the Phalanx marched along, throughout the entire line there was moſt vociferous applauſe. The enthuſiaſm along the route of march was poſitively unbounded, and teſtified not only to the popular approbation of the military bearing of the Corps, but alſo to the Patriotic ſympathies and aſſociations which its *tout enſemble* inſpired. The Phalanx reached the Monument grounds at eleven o'clock. For an hour or more before their arrival the grounds were thronged with a large concourſe of Citizens from Charleſtown and Boſton, a goodly portion being ladies. Among the diſtinguiſhed gentlemen preſent were *Commodore* Armſtrong, *Capt.* Hudſon (Commander of the Navy Yard,) *Hon.* Richard Frothingham, Jr., *Hon.* George Waſhington Warren, *Adjt. Gen.* Stone, and ſeveral members of the City Government of Charleſtown.

After marching around the Monument the Companies halted on the north-eaſt ſide of the ſhaft, where a ſquare was formed.

Captain Boyd, of the City Guard, then introduced His Honor *Mayor* Dana of Charleſtown, who proceeded to ſpeak as follows:

[In accordance with a vote of the Phalanx, the Secretary wrote to *Mayor* Dana for a reviſed copy of his ſpeech of welcome, which he ſent accompanied by a note in which he ſays: "The occaſion was one of much intereſt to our Citizens and will mark an era in our Hiſtory. I aſſure you that we appreciate the honor you have paid to our City, in your patriotic pilgrimage to the ſhrine of Bunker Hill. The opportunity of making ſo many pleaſant acquaintances, we regard as among the moſt happy features of the day. We ſhall watch the hiſtory of your Aſſociation with much intereſt; and ſhall not doubt that it will accompliſh the objects and purpofes fo happily alluded to by one of your diftinguifhed affociates."]

MAYOR DANA'S WELCOME.

Mr. Commander, Officers and Members of the Putnam Phalanx: In behalf of the Municipal Authorities and of our Citizens, it gives me great pleafure to welcome you to this Monumental City, and this hallowed fpot—the foil of Bunker Hill.

We are proud to welcome to our City a noble body of men fo largely reprefenting the intelligence, the moral worth, the profeffional, commercial, mercantile, manufacturing, mechanical, and induftrial interefts of our fifter State—the good old State of Connecticut—the land of a People proud in the purfuit and fruits of honeft induftry, and more proud of the Great Deeds of their Sires in thofe Colonial ftruggles which tried their fouls almoft as much as that great and final Struggle which fecured to you and to us the uncounted Political bleffings we enjoy. We refpect the pride which you feel as fons of a State which nearly one hundred years before the war of our Revolution, taking a bold and noble ftand above her Sifter Colonies, fcorned and defied the edicts of an unprincipled, cruel and tyrannical ruler, and by the hands of the intrepid Wadfworth refcued from the minions of the King her ancient Charter, and fecured it in that noble Oak, whofe fame will live while a defcendant of Wyllys remains to mark the Spot where it ftood. Sir, you do not come up to this confecrated Pile as ftrangers. Your Fathers came up here on the 17th of June, 1775, and fide by fide with our Fathers, fought that great Battle, the direct refult of which was the Independence of the Colonies and the Liberty of the Nation. As our Fathers on that great Day welcomed your Fathers, fo do we, the fons of Maffachufetts, on this aufpicious Day, now welcome you, the fons of Connecticut, to this facred Spot. Here, ftanding at the bafe of that noble Shaft, which commemorates the valor and the deeds of your Anceftry and of ours, let us vow, as our Fathers did, to ftand by and protect each other, againft foreign foes, or traitors at home, and let us rejoice that we have that great inftrument, our Conftitution, our common Shield, which it is our privilege to fupport and maintain. You come to us, fir, under a name ever hallowed, ever venerated. If New Hampfhire fent her Stark, and Maffachufetts her WARREN and her PRESCOTT, Connecticut fent her great Captain, whofe name you bear, PUTNAM, the Hero of two wars—the man who feared God and loved his country. Where, if not on this Hill, fhall the memory of Putnam be held in reverence? Who more than he fhared the generous confidence of Wafhington—who, more than He, infpired and encouraged the hearts of the Army? Who, more than he—and let me fay it with all refpect to the memory of all the noble Heroes of that great day—contributed to the fuccefsful refult of the Battle of Bunker Hill? While Maffachufetts claims the honor of his birthplace, his name and reputation are fafe in the keeping of his adopted State. Look around you, Sir, and behold yonder hills where ftood the Redoubt which quite encircled our fifter City. Much of this was built under the direction of your great Captain, who commanded the centre divifion of the Army, which was ftationed near Wafhington's headquarters. Look upon the Barrell Farm, where ftands Cobble Hill, upon which was the fortification built by Gen. Putnam. Look here upon this Hill, the fcene of his labors through the eventful Night of the 16th of June. Here ftands a part of the Fortification which he with his own hands affifted in conftructing on that fame night. On that corner of this Square he uttered thofe memorable words, "Wait till you fee the whites of their eyes. Take aim at their waiftbands!" In your ranks, we are told, runs the blood of Putnam and thofe other Heroes who ferved under or with him. Their memories are a rich Legacy to be poffeffed by you.

The *Major Commandant* introduced *Affiftant Commiffary* Deming, who refponded to the Mayor's welcome, as follows:

ASSISTANT COMMISSARY DEMING'S SPEECH AT BUNKER HILL.

Mr. Mayor, Officers of the City Government and Citizens of Charleftown: The Battalion which has intruded upon your hofpitality this morning is compofed, as your Honor has intimated, of perfons in every walk of life. Though effentially Military, and conforming to the rules which generally govern a Military Corps, and ready on any emergency to arm for the common defenfe and general welfare, it has other aims, not incompatible, I think, with its martial character. We aim to perpetuate by fuch fignificant memorials as its Drefs, its Name, its Mufic, and its Drill, an important part of the Hiftoric antecedents of old Connecticut. For a name, we go back to that Warrior-born, who, for fo long a period, infpired and marfhaled the warlike energies of the State. Our Drefs we have ventured to pattern exactly after that coftume (ftill preferved in the Patent Office at Wafhington,) which was worn by the Father of his Country; we march only to Revolutionary mufic; and our drill is, effentially, the fame which the Baron Steuben taught the Connecticut levies in the Camps of the Revolution — the fame, too, I believe, which was difplayed when Burgoyne furrendered his haughty fword — the fame, I know, under which our diftreffed Platoons tracked with their bloody feet the fnows of Valley Forge — the fame which carried the formidable battlements of Stoney Point, and which was fatal to Cornwallis and his myrmidons at Yorktown's clofing fight. Before our Organization was complete, before, certainly, we could boaft of any perfection in our drill, we refolved on a Pilgrimage of Patriotifm to this Holy Mount which witneffed the magnificent opening of the Revolutionary drama. As on the memorable 17th of June our Fathers and yours ftood here, fhoulder to fhoulder, intenfely fraternized by a common peril, it is fitting and proper, as you have intimated, Mr. Mayor, that upon the fame Spot their Sons fhould fraternize in common joy, at a common deliverance and a joint inheritance redeemed. You have been pleafed, Sir, to call our attention to the fortified eminences which encircle this fpot, to Ploughed Hill, Winter Hill, and Profpect Hill where the morning after the engagement *Col.* DANIEL PUTNAM found his father engaged in throwing up another Redoubt and Breaftwork in the pathway of the difpirited foe. But we wifh, Mr. Mayor, to be made more familiar with the field upon which we ftand. The topography of this fpot has been fo changed by the march of improvement, that we who have ftudied it from books alone, find difficulty in difcovering the precife points of this large expanfe confecrated by the courage and the blood of the Connecticut Detachments. Here, if I am correctly informed, on the fite of this towering Obelifk was the Redoubt which firft partitioned off this hallowed Spot from common earth and gave it to Hiftory, and there, parallel with its eaftern face, ftretched off a hundred yards towards the north the famous Breaftwork. But our Connecticut eyes, Mr. Mayor, fearch with more eagernefs for the Fences ftuffed with hay that covered the large area, between the termination of the Breaftwork and the banks of the Myftic, where KNOWLTON and CLARK and KEYS and CLEVELAND and our brave Three

Hundred stood, and GROSVENOR was wounded, and whose stout resistance saved the party in the Redoubt from instantaneous extermination and covered its retreat when the powder here was exhausted. We seek that Golgotha, on the summit of Bunker Hill over which *Capt.* CHESTER advanced, with his Company, towards the close of the engagement; we seek for the Valley of the Shadow of Death into which *Lieut.* WEBB descended, "and had no more thought of ever rising the hill again, than of ascending to heaven as Elijah did, soul and body together." We seek the terrible Neck enfiladed by the enemy's frigates, where passed backward and forward our heroic Leader bearing the trembling Reinforcements over it on the wings of his ever resplendent courage. It is to these points, Mr. Mayor, accepting those kind proffers of information which you have tendered, that our attention would be turned, that we may tread silently, slowly, and reverently there as among the Graves of our Household.

We are happy to be met, Mr. Mayor, by the Chief Executive of the City that guards the Shrine of our pilgrimage, with such cordial words of welcome and profuse proffers of hospitality; for both, I am directed by our Major Commandant, to offer our most grateful acknowledgments, and in return, to tender to the city of Charlestown our best wishes for its continued prosperity, and, that the foot of a foreign invader may never again desecrate its soil, and last but not least, to wish for yourself personally, Sir, both in your public walks and private relations, as Magistrate and Man, every felicity.

I was introduced to you, Sir, as the Commissary of the Phalanx, and the duty of Commissary, according to Steuben tactics, is to furnish supplies to the body: the Judge Advocate is Commissary to the Soul; and I should hardly have ventured to step out of my department into his, were it not to relieve him, temporarily, of the onerous duties in his peculiar line still impending over him to-day. We have also immediate use for his eloquent tongue. Before we left Hartford it was expected that he would improve the occasion while we stood on this suggestive Earth, to refreshen our Patriotism by some of those words of his, "that bear the spirit of great deeds winged to the Future." You will, therefore, pardon me, Mr. Mayor, if I anticipate any farther ceremonies which may await us here, by now introducing to you and the audience Judge Advocate Stuart, who will address his Companions in arms.

JUDGE ADVOCATE STUART'S ADDRESS AT BUNKER HILL.

Major-Commandant, and Officers and Soldiers of the Putnam Phalanx:—We ftand upon that ever-memorable Spot, where, at the outbreak of the American Revolution, in the firft battle-twilight of a new ftar dawning upon American hopes, fifteen hundred of the raw Yeomanry of our land, with a coolnefs and precifion of aim that are almoft unexampled,—twice, with their deadly fire of fmall arms, precipitated a veteran Britifh force of twice their number, in diforder and affright, with more than One Thoufand of their dead and wounded left upon the Field of Strife, back to their landing-place upon Moreton's Point! We ftand upon the very ground which thefe gallant Yeomen left their hold upon only when their failing ammunition compelled the ftep, and when their Redoubt was half-filled with the troops of the foe—troops whom, even though environed by them, they clubbed with their mufkets, as ftill undifmayed—unconquered, though retiring—and agonized only by the thought of their want of powder to continue the ftrife, they moved fternly away.

How ftartling, Gentlemen, muft have been the Scene—as we cannot but recall it here—aye, majeftic and tremendous,—with its blaze of more than five hundred buildings in Charleftown, the tall fteeple of the Meeting-Houfe in their midft itfelf forming a lofty Pyramid of flame—with all this added to the continual blaze and roar of Artillery! Scene too painfully touching from the attendant lofs of the pure, the brave, the accomplifhed, the high-fouled WARREN! Scene, however, to us of this Phalanx, fource alfo of pride; for here—confpicuous in every part of the Engagement, pervading and goading every part of it with his own ever-daring fpirit—was the Hero whofe name we bear, —the exhauftlefs, indomitable PUTNAM! And with him, from the State from which we come, were Captain KNOWLTON and Major DURKEE. With him were Captain CHESTER, and Captain CLARK, and Captain COIT. With him were Lieutenants DANA, GROSVENOR, and WEBB. With him was Enfign, afterwards General HENRY CHAMPION, the nobly patriotic Grandfather of our own equally patriotic Affiftant Commiffary DEMING. With him were SMITH and LOVEJOY, the two Grandfathers, on the paternal and maternal fide, of him the ftalwart and patriotic Standard-Bearer of this our battalion; and BILLINGS and HIBBARD, the two paternal and maternal Grandparents, alfo, of our Sergeant BILLINGS; and HIDE, the brave anceftor of our Private,

SHARP; and KEYES, and CLEVELAND, and KEMP, and BASSETT, and BINGHAM, and other gallant fpirits, many in number, from old Connecticut: — here they were, fide by fide and fhoulder to fhoulder, with intrepid Soldiery from Maffachufetts and intrepid Soldiery from New-Hampfhire, devoting themfelves, one and all, with patriotic fury to the bloody ftrife.

Unfortunate though the refult of this Battle, under one afpect — that of the enforced retreat — yet under another and loftier view, the Refult was moft propitious. For — for the firft time — it taught America her ftrength when oppofed in arms to the mighty Monarchy of England. It inoculated and fired her Spirit with confidence. It lured to the future Fight. It wiped off forever that reproach of timidity which had been flung upon her Troops. It taught Britifh foldiers to refpect, aye and to dread her martial Ability — at leaft behind entrenchments; and it taught Britifh Commanders-in-chief, and the haughty Cabinet of England, that military conflagrations would not anfwer in the New World.

The battle of Quebec — one far lefs deftructive of human life than that of Bunker Hill — gave to Great Britain the whole region of the St. Lawrence. That upon this fpot loft to Great Britain a Territory worth a dozen Canadas — loft to her Thirteen Colonies of proportions that were coloffal, and of capacities that have proved magnificent. For the Conteft waged upon the little arena here, developed a fpirit of Patriotifm fo pure — fo ardent — fo fearlefs — fo inflexible — fo energetic — fo irrepreffible — that it was fure to burn on by force of its own quenchlefs elemental Fire, until it had burned all tyranny off from the field of ftruggling America — until its own ethereal Light had chafed from our new trans-Atlantic expanfe every fhadow even of vaffalage to any potentate on Earth — and left it bathed in the full effulgence of Life, Liberty, and Independence.

In that Effulgence we this day ftand — and upon the very Altar where the Light which formed it was firft kindled. Juft mark it, then, for an inftant, Soldiers — and you, if you pleafe, the Spectators of this fcene, whofe attentive intereft is moft grateful to our Corps — mark that Effulgence of which I fpeak, from this Standpoint — as it appears in the profperity of our country fince the time when the blood of the earlieft Martyrs to the Revolution was here fhed.

Behold our Population rifen from three to near thirty millions — our Towns and Cities, from comparatively a few, to thofe which are numberlefs! Witnefs the magic converfion of the Ohio and Miffouri folitudes to civilized Homes — while far beyond — threading the thoufand devious arms of the Miffiffippi — afcending the broad declivities of the Rocky Mountains — climbing tortuous crags — winding through treacherous canons — and ploughing terrific fnows — fearlefs Emigrants have pufhed on to liften to the favage whoop on the banks of the Columbia, and the Sacramento, and to found and rear Inftitutions and Temples, to Liberty and to God, within found of the breaking billow on the very fhore of the Pacific! Everywhere almoft over our land, liften to the elaftic fteam — hear the tramp of the Iron Horfe! Behold upon almoft all our waters the white fail! Mark Science and Art — Invention and Induftry — Knowledge and Education — everywhere almoft diffufed! Mark, in fhort, a National Happinefs, which, under all its afpects, is more profound than that of any other People on the face of the Earth — and which fpreads, over and around us — from fea to fea — a fun-illumined atmofphere, in which we all may chant the undying Songs and Alleluias of the Free!

To fuch a height of greatnefs has the Spirit of Patriotifm — which difplayed itfelf upon this Spot — in June, 1775 — exalted our country. A Spirit, therefore, it was, it is obvious, of no common mould — no mere, naked, uninformed natural impulfe — but it was an impulfe feafoned by Knowledge — it was enlightened by Forefight. It comprehended a rich and vaft throng of affociations derived from a long experience of Civilization. It underftood clearly the danger to all the civil, focial, and domeftic relations of the Colonies involved in the tyrannous claims of England. It knew well the inexhauftible refources of the New World — and forefaw its rifing greatnefs in the funfhine of Peace. And it therefore toiled at the battle of Bunker Hill — not alone for the America of the Revolution — but for the America of all time. It fought that fight in order that the People whom it infpired might not only glorioufly vindicate their own fundamental Rights, but plant for Pofterity, as well as for themfelves — fet beyond even the tornado's power — that Tree of Liberty whofe is the golden fruitage of a National Civilization, Happinefs, and Glory, which, it was hoped, would endure Forever.

To a fpirit of Patriotifm thus pure — thus heroic — thus enlightened — here upon this Spot, its early home — its blood-ftained Altar, but not, thank God, its Grave — here then let us all bend in reverence, as to the Mecca of our Civil Faith — our Tutelary Shrine — the tryfting-place of our Republican love—here let us bend, and from its inspiration drink deep draughts!

Calling to us from the bones of those Patriots who here immolated their lives—pointing to us with a finger blazing as of sapphire from their Tombs—this Spirit bids us love the Land that gave us birth. The Laws that protect you, it says—the Institutions which form you—the Customs you obey—the Habits in which you take comfort—the Home Histories, and dear Traditions, and Legends, in which you rejoice—*these are your Country.*

The Skies you see above you—that Earth you gaze upon beneath—those sweet spots upon its surface, especially, where you drew the first luscious breath of life, and were hushed by the soft-flowing lullabies of Home—the Waters that cover that natal Earth—the living things that dwell upon it—the sustenance it yields—the fruits with which it abounds—the Songs with which it is vocal—*these are your Country.*

The Villages, the Towns, the Cities you inhabit—the family loves you cherish—the pious devotions to which you cling—the social ties you bind—the anxieties you indulge—the sorrows you feel—the hopes you warm into life—the Good Deeds you perform, and those accomplished by your fellows—the Good Names you establish, and those established around you—*these are your Country.*

Your Country it is that wrapped its folds around you when first you saw the light. With its loving folds it has encircled you ever since—and it will enshroud you gently with them when you die.

Make your Country, then, the idol of your heart,—Cherish it in your heart of hearts. Should it acquire new honors, glory in them. Should it receive wounds—which Heaven forefend—approach them as you would the wounds of a Parent—" with pious awe, and trembling solicitude," and tenderest ministration. Die for your Country, should peril ever require the sacrifice!

Thus, Soldiers of the Phalanx—thus does the Spirit of Patriotism appeal to us from this hallowed Spot. Pray God, we may all respond to the appeal! Pray God, the shadows of the Patriots who here offered up their lives may float ever through our Households! Allying ourselves ever closely to them—"the boldest and most noble Men of Progress that the World has ever seen"—may we ally *them*, through us, to Generations yet to come—ourselves, in the sublime language of that immortal Man who here inaugurated the rudimental

Corner-Stone of this proud Monument, "being but links in that great chain of being which beginning with the origin of our Race, runs onward through its fucceffive Generations, binding together the Paft, the Prefent, and the Future, and terminating at laft, with the confummation of all things Earthly, at the Throne of God!"

The Chaplain of the Battalion, *Rev.* Afher Moore, then offered the following folemn and impreffive

Prayer.

God of our Fathers! Ruler among the Nations! And Judge of all the Earth! We reverently bow before Thee at this facred Shrine of our Country's Liberty, devoutly thanking Thee for the ineftimable bleffings that have come to us through the toils and treafures and blood of the incorruptible Patriots who fecured to us the pricelefs gift of National Independence!

Here, Almighty God, may we gratefully call to our remembrance the valorous Deeds of our revered Fathers, who refolutely confronted the foes of Liberty in the day of trial, and nobly "jeoparded their lives unto the Death in the high places of the Field!" Here may our Patriotifm receive frefh Infpiration! Here may unborn Generations come in Pilgrim troops to offer a Nation's gratitude to the Giver of all bleffings! And here may the hearts of our Children be cemented in that *Union* which made our Fathers ftrong in the day of dreadful deeds!

Lord, blefs our common Country! Preferve us from divifions and ftrife. Let Peace reft upon our Land, and Profperity abound throughout all our borders. Forgive us our fins. And with us blefs all the Nations of the Earth, through Jefus Chrift, our Lord! *Amen.*

Mayor Dana then introduced the *Hon.* George Wafhington Warren, who, as Prefident of the Monument Affociation, welcomed the Phalanx to Bunker Hill.

Hon. Richard Frothingham, Jr., *ex-Mayor* of Charlestown, introduced by *Mayor* Dana, commenced by remarking on the furpaffing intereft of the fcene, and its fuggeftive character—fuggeftive of the time when Connecticut and Maffachufetts ftood together. To fhow the fpirit of Connecticut then, an incident was related of the times of the Port Bill, when Bofton and Charleftown felt heavy the hand of power. No Colony was more prompt to fend material aid, and accompany it with folemn pledges, than Connecticut; and one cafe was inftanced where Putnam brought on a drove of fheep, and with them a letter addreffed to Bofton, having his Signature. It reads that the men of Connecticut meant firft to attempt to appeafe the fire of a vindictive Miniftry by the blood of rams and of lambs, and if this did not anfwer, they were ready to march in the Van and fprinkle American altars with their hearts' blood, if it were neceffary. That was the fpirit of the brave old Hero who figned this letter, and the fpirit of Knowlton, and Chefter, and Webb, and Durkee, and all the gallant Men who here made good the pledge.

The fpecial duty affigned the Connecticut Forces in the Bunker Hill action was then particularly defcribed, and having delineated the main Pofitions at about two o'clock in the afternoon, and the work then going on, the reafon was ftated why the Connecticut Forces were ordered out from the Redoubt to prevent this pofition being furrounded; the location of the Rail Fence which they commenced and Starks men completed, and the gallant and vital Service rendered here, were dwelt upon; and then the fpot, Bunker Hill, was pointed to where, on the retreat, Putnam fo heroically tried to rally the men anew. In concluding, the fentiment was expreffed that fifter States of fo glorious a renown as Connecticut and Maffachufetts could have no other rivalry than rivalry in the Works of Progrefs that adorn Society,— in Education, Commerce, Induftry—in the determination to protect and defend the pricelefs Inheritance of Liberty won by the ftruggles and blood of fuch Anceftry as fought at Bunker Hill. This Addrefs was warmly applauded throughout.

The exercifes at the Monument occupied about two hours.

Immediately after Mr. Frothingham's remarks the City Guard efcorted the Phalanx to the Guard's Armory, where a bountiful Collation was ferved, to which ample juftice was done—while *Mayor* Dana alfo entertained the Battalion and a large number of invited guefts, in a fumptuous manner, at his refidence, in Monument fquare, and Mr. Frothingham received at his refidence the Officers and Staff. At thefe places brief Speeches were made by *Mayor* Dana, *ex-Mayor* Frothingham, *Commiffary* Deming, *Paft Commander* Pierce of the Charleftown City Guard, and others. At half-paft one o'clock the line was re-formed on Winthrop ftreet, and marched to the Charleftown Navy Yard.

VISIT TO THE NAVY YARD.

On their arrival at the Charleftown Navy Yard, the Phalanx were received, on entering the gates, by a Detachment of fixty Marines under the command of *Lieutenant* Reynolds, who were drawn up in open order and prefented arms as the Battalion paffed through. The Battalion was alfo honored with a National Salute of thirty-one guns. Thefe matters are note-worthy, fince the Phalanx is the firft Military Organization which was ever received at the Navy Yard with fimilar honors—indeed, the firft that was ever permitted to march in bearing arms. Paffing the Marines, the Phalanx was drawn up before Head-Quarters where they were received by *Capt.* Hudfon, Commandant of the ftation, and other Naval Officers. *Capt.* Hudfon welcomed the Phalanx briefly as follows:

Major Commandant and Members of the Putnam Phalanx: I welcome you to the Navy Yard, and fhould be moft happy to fhow you whatever of intereft may be upon the premifes. I am no fpeech-maker—only a plain Sailor; but when I fee a body of Soldiers dreffed in the uniform of the venerated Wafhington, it touches me with an emotion that it is difficult adequately to exprefs. The present generation can fcarcely imagine the fufferings of their Fathers in that Revolutionary ftruggle; they battled as it were with the halter around their necks; they fuffered, and we now enjoy the Fruits of their Labors. But it is not my intention to make a fpeech; I will only repeat to you, *Major Commandant and Soldiers,* my cordial welcome to the Charleftown Navy Yard.

Judge Advocate Stuart, on being introduced by the *Major Commandant* of the Phalanx, refponded as follows:

Commodore Hudson:—For the cordial manner in which you welcome the Putnam Phalanx to this Navy Yard, I return you, in behalf of its Members, their heartfelt thanks. You very modeftly announce yourfelf as no Speech-maker—as only "a plain Sailor"—unhabituated to the fluent language of formal oratory. Sir, in my judgment, you have juft now made one of the happieft of all Speeches, for you have uttered to us, who, moftly, are ftrangers to thefe premifes, fweet Words of Welcome, that are warm from a Sailor's generous heart—a heart, proverbially, open as the broad expanfe of Sea.

And, Sir, we of this Phalanx, fhall take great pleafure in accepting your kind invitation to view the Spot which you fo ably fuperintend, and which, as we glance over it from our Stand-point here, bears unequivocal marks of intelligent Care, and contains ftriking and grateful evidences of the Strength and Greatnefs of our Country's Naval Power.

We from Connecticut take efpecial pride in this Naval Power, and in the fpectacle of it here. For, *Commodore,* within the waters of our State—in the capacious and beautiful harbor of our own City of New London—was fitted out the very firſt Naval Squadron of the United States that ever ſailed under the flag of our Common Country. That little Squadron conſiſted of the *Alfred*, the *Columbus*, the *Andrea Doria*, and the *Cabot*, varying in armament from fourteen to ſixteen guns. *Governor* Trumbull, Senior—that "rebel" Governor of our State, of world-wide fame—was the zealous and effective Patriot who, chiefly, aided to fit it out—and when made ready, it ſailed, in 1776, from the waters of New London harbor upon the firſt Naval Expedition ever made under the authority of Congreſs.

Yes, worthy *Commodore*—and into the waters of this harbor again, it brought back the Firſt-fruits of our firſt Revolutionary ſtruggle upon the Great Deep—and theſe Fruits, thank Heaven, triumphant ones! For *Admiral* Eſek Hopkins, its Commander-in-chief, ſailed with his new and infant Squadron to the Iſland of Abacco, lying near New Providence, in the Weſt India ſeas. And there he captured the *Governor* of this Iſland, and its *Deputy Governor*, and one of its *Councillors*, and ſeventy other Britiſh ſubjects—together with forty cannon, and fifteen braſs mortars, and a Britiſh ſchooner, and a Bermudian ſloop—and to theſe Prizes adding, on his paſſage home, a Britiſh bomb brig laden with arms, which he took near the end of Long Iſland, he ſailed triumphantly back, as I have juſt ſuggeſted, into that harbor of Connecticut from which he ſtarted. And thoſe cannon to which I refer, and that captured ſloop, were at once, with the conſent and approbation of Congreſs, applied by our ceaſeleſſly enterpriſing *Governor* to the Naval Service ſpecially of Connecticut, and generally of our whole Country.

Deep indeed then, and grateful, is the intereſt which this Phalanx feels in the preſent flouriſhing condition of this extenſive National Maritime Depot. It has grown up from a Navy which had its birth, and whoſe infancy was nurſed, in our own old Connecticut—and whoſe manhood—in that Second War which ſealed the triumphs and the independence of the Firſt—was adorned by a ſon of Connecticut in whom you, Sir, and all of us, take juſt pride—the Hero of *Old Ironſides, Commodore* Hull.

What a contraſt does this Yard now preſent to the aſpect which marked it years ago! When the ſtartling Fight took place upon that memorable, overlooking Height which we have juſt viſited, it was trodden by the foot of War, and ſtrewn with the carcaſes of the ſlain.

A rough, wild fpot it was then, bordered with unfightly marfhes, and with not a trace of tillage. Now it is a level, embellifhed, folid area, with every adaptation that fkill can contrive for a magnificent Naval Depot. Its appearance, in every refpect, Commodore, reflects the higheft credit upon your fuperintending care, and affures us all that the glorious Flag which waves above it will never, in hands fuch as your own, receive anything but additional Luftre.

And now, Sir, thanking you again, heartily, for your kind reception, and for the honors and privileges you accord, our Battalion will march, as you defire, around this Yard, and then take its leave.

At the conclufion of *Judge Advocate* Stuart's refponfe to *Capt.* Hudfon, the Phalanx vifited the various objects of intereft in the Navy Yard. On leaving, the Phalanx were again faluted by the Marines. On their return to Bofton at 3 o'clock, the Battalion paffed through State ftreet, which was literally crowded with people, and the appearance of the Phalanx was the fignal for loud and long continued applaufe. From State ftreet they proceeded direct to Summer ftreet, to the refidence of *Hon.* Edward Everett, in front of which they halted, and were drawn up in order. Mr. Everett was received by the Battalion with a military falute, after which *Capt.* Boyd introduced Mr. Everett to *Major* Goodwin, and the Commandant introduced Mr. Everett to the Battalion. Mr. Everett then fpoke as follows:

Address of Mr. Everett.

Mr. Commander and Gentlemen of the Putnam Phalanx:—I beg you to accept my grateful acknowledgments for the honor of this Salute. A compliment of this kind, ufually paid only to thofe in high Office, or marked out as acceptants of the public favor, muft be confidered a very diftinguifhed attention, by a perfon like myfelf, wholly withdrawn from Public Life.

I do not, however, require a perfonal honor of this kind, to lead me to fhare the gratification which your vifit affords to our Community. The character of the Company has gone before you. Conspicuous as individuals among the substantial Citizens of Hartford, you cannot but command respect as Members of this, for many reasons, remarkable Corps. You have already received ample assurance that I do but echo the general sentiment, in bidding you cordially Welcome to Boston.

The friends of the Militia system are gratified that it is receiving the countenance,— that it is strengthened by the participation,— of Citizens like those who compose the Putnam Phalanx. That system was long ago pronounced by John Adams one of the four pillars of the prosperity of New England. In the opinion of that eminent and sagacious Statesman and Patriot, the Volunteer Militia was entitled to be placed by the side of the Church, the School-house, and the Municipal Organizations of New England, as one of the main elements of the public Welfare and Safety.

Our fathers relied upon the Militia as a substitute for Standing Armies, which they considered as dangerous to the Liberties of the People. So great was the aversion entertained to a large standing Military Force in time of Peace, that, in the Federal Convention, it was proposed as an article of the Constitution that there never should be a standing Army of more than five thousand men. After this proposition had been debated for some time, General Washington rose, and great anxiety was felt to know what view would be taken by him of this proposal to place a Constitutional limit to the Standing Military Force of the Country. He simply moved an amendment to the article, adding the further provision that no invading Army should ever exceed three thousand.

Gentlemen, I hope and believe that a long time will elapse before the soil of the Union will be trod by an invading Army, great or small; few things, I think, are less likely to happen. Should such an event ever take place, I need not say that the main reliance of the Country for its protection and defence will not be on a standing Army. To withdraw from Commerce, Agriculture, and Manufactures, a sufficient number of men to station at every accessible point in our vast Territory a standing Military Force competent to face the enormous Armies of Europe, is manifestly impossible. Our defensive establishment on land will, for a long time, as now, consist of a moderate regular Force: a body of well trained Officers, reared at an admirable Military School; an ample supply of arms placed in the hands of the

People; fortifications at the vulnerable points, and then this all-pervading net-work of railroads by which, in twenty-four hours, a hundred thoufand of the Citizen Soldiery of the Country can be affembled at the point of danger.

Mr. Commander and Gentlemen, I anticipate no fuch Crifis; but if, among the poffibilities of the Future, it fhould arife, the fpirit which animates your Corps, pervading the mafs of our Fellow-citizens, will prove itfelf equal to any emergency.

You come among us under circumftances which befpeak a hearty Welcome. You have adopted the old Continental Organization. Your uniform is that which Wafhington wore; your mufic is the fimple drum and fife—no other was heard at Lexington, Concord and Bunker Hill. Your name is one which Maffachufetts, to the lateft generation, will delight to honor—that of the yeoman Soldier, who never looked back but once after putting his hand to the plow, and that was when he left it in the furrow, at the tidings of Lexington and Concord. You fhare, I doubt not, his fpirit, and in the hour of danger would imitate his example.

But other duties, other calls await you. Again tendering you, *Mr. Commander and Gentlemen,* my cordial thanks for this diftinguifhed honor, and wifhing you a fafe return to your Homes, I bid you a refpectful Farewell.

In reply to Mr. Everett's addrefs, which was warmly applauded, *Judge Advocate* Stuart, in behalf of the Phalanx, refponded as follows:

Hon. Mr. Everett: The Battalion now before you, from Hartford, Connecticut, known as the Putnam Phalanx, in teftimony of its refpect for you, Sir, as one of the moft diftinguifhed Sons of America, calls to give you greeting—and for the cordial manner, and eloquent, inftructive remarks, with which you have received us, it returns its heartfelt thanks.

We are organized for the purpose of aiding to revive and ftrengthen thofe glorious Memories of the Revolution to which you, Sir, efpecially through your fignal portraiture of the Father of his Country, have confecrated a liberal fhare of your time and your genius. By wearing, as we do, the military drefs of the Revolutionary times—

and this Drefs modeled with exactnefs from that of Wafhington himfelf, which is preferved in the Capitol of our country — by an adoption, in good part, of the tactics which prevailed in Wafhington's Army — through the Drum and Fife as the fole inftruments of Mufic — and by other conformities to ufages in the Times that tried Men's Souls — it is our aim to ftimulate a patriotic refpect for that great Revolution which made us free, and to awaken love and admiration for the Heroes who achieved it.

At the head of thefe Heroes — "Firft in Peace" — to ufe phrafes of familiar but ever endeared characterization — "Firft in Peace, firft in War, and firft in the hearts of his fellow Countrymen," — ftands that immortal Man whofe character and conduct you have yourfelf portrayed with mafterly difcrimination, with loving tendernefs, and in colors of light. In a fpirit of true Patriotifm, with fagacious forefight, and with lofty zeal, you have magnanimoufly devoted this Delineation to the noble purpofe of preferving entire and inviolate — for a Nation's veneration, for all time — the Home and the Tomb of Wafhington. For this end your labors have been unwearied. They have extended over a large part of the Union. Crowded audiences have hung upon your lips; their purfe, if not lavifh, has been generous towards your object; you have added many thoufands of dollars to the facred Mount Vernon Fund.

For this, Sir, you have a Nation's thanks. For this, the Ladies of our Land outpour their gratitude, and Men echo your praife. For this, Pofterity will rife up and call you "Bleffed!" And for this, the Putnam Phalanx — on this fpecial occafion — here at the door of your own dwelling — defires to exprefs its grateful acknowledgments. It is our ardent wifh and hope that your future Labors in the fame direction, fhould they be continued, may be crowned with eminent Succefs; that you may long live to behold the Home of the Father of his Country poffeffed, adorned, and perpetuated as Public Property, and be gratified by the fpectacle of frefh devotion, roufed, the whole country through, to his Memory, and to the Memories of all our Revolutionary Sires.

It is our ardent wifh, in your own fublimely expreffive language upon another occafion, that all "the grand Sympathies of Country, and that myftic tiffue of Race, woven far back in the dark chambers of the Paft, which, after the viciffitudes and migrations of Centuries, wraps up Great Nations in its broad mantle, and thofe fignificant expreffions,

Forefather, Parent, Child, Pofterity, Native Land, which carry volumes of meaning in a word"— it is our hope that all thefe may teach us — and teach our Countrymen everywhere—"not blindly to worfhip, but duly to honor the Paft; to ftudy the leffons of Experience; to fcan the high Counfels of man in his great Affociations; in Laws, in Maxims, in Traditions, in thofe great undoubted Principles of Right and Wrong which are fanctioned by the general confent of Mankind; thus tracing in human Inftitutions fome faint reflection of that Divine Wifdom, which fafhioned the Leaf that unfolded itfelf but a few weeks ago in the Foreft, after the pattern of the Leaf that was bathed in the dews of Paradife on the morning of the Creation."

With this expreffion of our fentiments, and renewedly thanking you for the courteous reception you have given us, this Phalanx now bids you a cordial and refpectful Adieu.

At the conclufion of this refponfe, feveral of the members of the Phalanx were introduced to Mr. Everett, after which the Companies proceeded to the parade ground of the Common. The attendance on the Common was immenfe. Every available fpot outfide the lines was occupied by the eager Crowd, and a large number of Ladies and Gentlemen were admitted by ticket within the lines.

At half-paft four o'clock, the Second Battalion of Infantry, numbering 86 guns, under command of *Major* Charles O. Rogers, accompanied by Gilmore's full Band and Drum Corps, left their Armory, and proceeded to the City Hall, where they received *Mayors* Lincoln of Bofton and Dana of Charleftown, together with members of both branches of the Government of each City, whom they efcorted to the Common. The Charleftown City Guard then took their leave of the Phalanx and marched for home. The line of the Phalanx was formed, and they were reviewed by *Mayors* Lincoln and Dana, *Alderman* Pierce, and J. Putnam Bradlee, Efq., *Prefident of the*

Council, of Bofton. While this review was progreffing, the Second Battalion marched to the State Houfe, where they received *Adjutant-General* Stone, *Brigadier-General* Bullock and Staff of the Firft Brigade, *Col.* Cowdin and Staff of the Second Regiment Infantry, and *Major* White and Staff of the Firft Battalion Cavalry, whom they efcorted to the Parade Ground. The above named Officers then reviewed the Phalanx. The Corps then paffed in Review before the Officers, marching to the foul-ftirring mufic of their own Drum Band. The marching of the Phalanx was loudly applauded by the affembled multitude. After the Review, the Second Battalion went through a drefs parade in excellent ftyle, after which both companies efcorted *Gen.* Stone and his Officers to the State Houfe. The line of march was then refumed, the Phalanx being efcorted through Beacon, School, Wafhington, Summer, Chauncy, Harrifon avenue, and Beach ftreets, to the United States Hotel, where they were difmiffed, the Second Battalion returning to their Armory.

In the evening, a large number of the Phalanx availed themfelves of the courteous invitation of Mr. E. L. Davenport, manager of the Howard Athenæum, and vifited that eftablifhment. *Mayor* Lincoln kept open houfe during the evening and hofpitably received the Phalanx. Oliver Ellfworth, Efq., a member of the Battalion, fumptuoufly entertained the entire Corps at his refidence, No. 21 Somerfet ftreet. This Re-union was one of the moft delightful and pleafant incidents of the entire Excurfion, and at the refidence of their Brother-member, the Phalanx were made to feel at home. During the evening, Geo. H. Clark, Efq., who was one of the guefts of the occasion, added materially to the enjoyments of the Festival by reading the following appropriate Poem:

It's just what I expected — and I cannot well complain: —
Because a fellow did it once you thought he would again:
And so, to meet the Challenger in case one should appear,
I brought a loaded gun along — you see I have it here!

I was busy with a Customer about a little bill,
With one eye on his pocket-book and one upon the till;
The gross amount was figured up — it wasn't very large —
And he had stirred me with his cry of "charge, Chester, charge!"

When steps me in a portly man who couldn't see his knee,
With a smile upon his lip, and said "I want you, Mr. C—."
I knew he was no Constable — those Caitiffs never smile —
And thus with words of blandishment my ear he did beguile.

"Our Phalanx, whose Ambition soars beyond a prosy Drill,
Is going on a Pilgrimage to famous Bunker Hill:
We mean to stand, with hat in hand, where glorious Putnam fought,
And tread the Soil where noble Deeds by him were nobly wrought.

We go with no inflamed desire, nor any sly intent
To bring away by force of Arms the Charlestown Monument: —
Although it were an easy thing to do so if we chose,
As every body who has seen the Putnam Phalanx knows.

And we want you to come along — we'll have a jovial time —
And don't forget to bring with you a pleasant bit of Rhyme.
The day is fixed for Tuesday next — no dodging for the rain —
And pray be prompt, because, you see, we're going on a Train!"

Well, here I am — a little man among top-booted screamers,
Like to a Clipper mid a fleet of huge Great Eastern Steamers;
A sort of rakish *Letter o' marque* beside my big Compeers —
So let my signals all be marked as meant for private ears.

I'm told your Mothers know you're out — how is it with your Wives?
And have the thoughtful Creatures got insurance on your Lives?

I truſt when you are ſafely back they'll aſk no idle queſtions,
To anſwer which would interfere with delicate digeſtions.

It has been ſometimes aſked of me, in quite a ſerious way,
If you in caſe of actual War would mingle in the Fray?
I anſwer Yes:—and what is more, no Danger would you ſhun,
For it is quite impoſſible that ſuch Great Men ſhould run!

No—be aſſured of this one thing, though large the target be,
A broadſide might rake down your ranks before a ſoul would flee:
Cocked hats might wilt, and breeches rip, and coats be rent and torn,
Yet ſtill amid the thickeſt Fight your Banner would be borne.

Look at the Standard Bearer there and doubt it if you can!
And think if thoſe odd legs would ſave our excellent Squire Mann!
And Deming too—the Enemy would make a deadly breach
In every thing his broadcloth hid, ere he the rear could reach.

The mental Courage that dilates each Soldier's flaſhing eye,
Would be excited by the fact that he muſt do or die.
So all ye bull-necked Britiſhers, beware theſe men of might,
Who wont ſurrender, cannot run—but Glory! how they'll fight!

You may talk about Thermopylaes and Marathons of old;
Of Lodi and of Waterloo, and all their Heroes bold;
I'll bet a ſcore of pumpkin pies, and help the party eat 'em,
That Major Goodwin and his troop would give 'em odds and beat 'em!

You've one might rank, if ſo he choſe, with old Demoſthenes;
And a lineal Son of that old Greek we call Thucydides;
And others who but bide their time to ſhow their fellow men
That they can wield, as Cæſar did, the Sword as well as Pen.

One member may his patients purge, and one may ſhove the plane;
And one may have an oily tongue and wag the ſame for gain.
You may have Merchants, Preſidents, and men from toil retired,
But all with warlike viſions now are moſt intenſely fired.

Your Colt would ſhoot a dozen foes the while the reſt were aiming;
And Aſhmead's hammer, like old Thor's, the cohorts would be maim-
    ing:

And Tiffany, when duty calls, will prove no terrapin,
But like a valiant Printer fend a frequent bullet in.

And where in cafe of a retreat, would neighbor Strong be found?
Dead — or like Falftaff feigning death — along the bloody ground!
And Sharp, his roadfters four in hand would never drive again,
But like a hunted Buffalo loom up among the flain.

Well, let us hope there'll be no War:— we're quiet loving folk —
And really, after all that's faid, this fighting is no joke.
I never liked the trade, myfelf, fince I was quite a lad,
When Billy Wolcott broke my head, and pummelled me fo bad.

We've come to vifit Bunker Hill. We've alfo come to dine.
We alfo mean to tafte a glafs of Bofton people's wine.
I wonder if they would have thrown fuch nectar in the Sea,
If George had taxed it as he did that plaguy lot of Tea!

What good things they to-day provide let us to-day difcufs —
For when another morning breaks they'll breakfaft upon us!
To-morrow they will furely have — dreffed up as "lateft news"—
A difh of Putnam Phalanx ferved, to flank their prandial ftews.

Ah — blefs thofe Editorial Chaps :— it is a way they've got,
Of feizing jokes, like buckwheat cakes, while they are piping hot;
And while the Jokers are abed, and dreaming of new feats,
Thofe Typos will be "fetting up"— and pulling off the fheets!

May you look back upon this day with Patriotic Pride,
And with a keener relifh ftill your ambling Hobby ride;
And may thofe folemn looking hats acquire no rakifh tricks,
Nor ever be a lurking place for fad convivial bricks!

At nine o'clock on Thurfday morning, the Phalanx were affembled preparatory to their departure for Providence. Notwithftanding the fatigues of the day previous, every man was in readinefs for Duty. The day was cool, with a high wind which rendered marching fomewhat uncomfortable. The Phalanx paraded a fhort time only on the Common, where it was expected that an Artift would photograph the Battalion, but the day was unfavorable for the operation. After a brief parade, the Battalion, accompanied by thoufands, marched to the Providence Depot. A large Crowd was affembled to witnefs their Departure, and as the Train left at eleven a. m., cheer after cheer was raifed for the Putnam Phalanx, which were returned moft heartily by the Battalion for their Bofton friends.

The members of the Phalanx retain the moft grateful and pleasant recollection of their brief but joyous vifit to Bofton and Charleftown. The Hofpitable Citizens of thofe places feem to have neglected no endeavor to honor the Phalanx with their admiration and attentions. The local Papers fpeak of their vifit as an event of no ordinary moment in their Cities' Hiftory. They eftimate the Crowds affembled to witnefs the Receptions and various Parades of the Battalion by "tens of thoufands." And it is pleafant to the Phalanx to put on Record permanently, the following fpontaneous expreffions of opinion from fome of the more prominent Daily Journals:

[From the Bofton Poft.]

For — well, we'll fay — forty years — we haven't felt fo much like playing truant to tag Soldiers about the ftreets as we did yefterday morning upon feeing the PUTNAM PHALANX paraded in front of the United States Hotel. Happy Hoftelry! to have breakfafted fuch a Squad — every one a folid Citizen with a good ftomach, every one a Gentleman, a Soldier and a Patriot; for, as a ftranger remarked to us, it ifn't poffible for fuch men to vote the fectional ticket. From the tall, venerable, white-haired and white-whifkered Commander down to the fhorteft Private, every one had the jaunty and genial air of a fmiling October morning in New England —

(Hail to the land whereon we tread!)

but under this peaceful exterior of yellow feathers it required no great imagination to perceive the daring of the Wolf-hunter whofe name they bear. We never faw, hereabout, any military thing finer than the eafe and grace of their movements as they formed and marched up Beach ftreet to the tune of "The Girl I left behind Me," played by their old-fafhioned Drum Corps with a mellow nicety that brought the tears into the eyes of a young Lady ftanding near us. Like her, forry to be left behind the fhowy Phalanx, we threw our head up and our fomewhat rounded fhoulders back, and marched down to the fcene of our accuftomed labors with as much of a military port as we could affume without appearing ridiculous, but feeling all the time that Athens is eclipfed, and the beft of our Battalions muft knock under to that of Hartford.

[From the Bofton Tranfcript.]

The Putnam Phalanx is an Organization for Social and Hiftoric as well as Military purpofes. Yet we have heard but one opinion expreffed in this City in regard to the Corps. Univerfal commendation of the fine, noble bearing of its Members, and praife of the general difcipline of the Battalion, have affigned to the Phalanx a higher place in the efteem of our Citizens, than that of any military Vifitors for a long feries of Years. Thefe caufes operate, however, in a military direction folely. But there are influences more potent, which have produced their effect upon Perfons, whofe habits of life and modes of thought do not predifpofe them to a love of martial Parade. Such agencies relate to the willingnefs of the people of Bofton to give intellectual and moral Worth its proper Pofition. That the Phalanx takes a front rank in the former regard is proved by the felicitous, and, in parts, eloquent Speeches of Hon. I. W. Stuart and H. C. Deming, Efq., made on Wednefday, on Bunker Hill and in Bofton. We are alfo affured that in a moral point of view the Battalion is no lefs entitled to refpect. The fame of fome on its Roll, as men of fubftance preceded their arrival here. We hope their vifit to this City was as productive of enjoyment to the entire memberfhip of the "Phalanx" as agreeable to our Community.

[From the Charleftown (Mafs.) Advocate.]

The Putnam Phalanx is about the moft fubftantial, and the jollieft looking Company of men that ever got together in this Town before. Hartford muft be a defolate looking place after permitting fuch a Body to quit its limits, to go in fearch of Honors upon foreign Fields — becaufe, no Town could by any poffibility, at leaft not in thefe days, fend out a Phalanx like them, and yet have enough left to keep up the dignity of the Place.

What a void their Wives and Children and Fellow-citizens muft experience without their prefence.—Some of the fineft fpecimens of phyfical manhood, and noblenefs of carriage and feature, could be felected from among them. A fculptor would not want for models among fuch a Crowd. He would be puzzled which to choofe. And many of them were men of "moft unbounded ftomach," ftout trencher men, before whom dyfpepfia, indigeftion, and melancholy would difappear as Shadows that vanifh at the approach of Morning. Looking at them, we felt an intenfe defire to fling up our beaver, and cry out "Hurrah for Connecticut!" if fhe manufactures wooden nutmegs, fhe don't fend abroad wooden men. Hurrah for Connecticut!

THE ARRIVAL AT PROVIDENCE.

At one o'clock p. m., Thurfday, Oct. 6th, a fignal gun from the battery of the Marine Artillery, which was ftationed near Canal ftreet, announced the approach of the Train from Bofton with the Putnam Phalanx. The fignal gun was followed by a National Salute of thirty-one guns, for which purpofe a detachment of twenty men, under the command of *Orderly Sergeant* George E. Brown, had been detailed by the acting Commander of the Marine Corps of Artillery, *Lieut. Col.* C. H. Tompkins. Near the Depot and on Exchange place, was a concourfe of thoufands of People who had affembled to greet the Phalanx and witnefs their Reception by the Firft Light Infantry and the Old Guard. By the beft of arrangements nearly the entire Square was kept open and referved for the Military. The formalities of reception and mutual introductions having taken place, the two Battalions took up the line of march, the Infantry efcorting their Guefts through Exchange, Weftminfter and Dorrance ftreets to the Infantry Armory, where an elegant collation was given to the Phalanx by their Hofts. *Col.* W. W. Brown briefly welcomed the Phalanx to the City, and *Major Commandant* Goodwin refponded. After an hour of focial intercourfe, the Battalions formed on Dorrance ftreet, in the following order:

American Brafs Band, J. C. Greene, leader, 20 pieces, in blue uniform.

Firft Light Infantry, *Col.* W. W. Brown, Commandant; Firft Company in fcarlet coats, numbering 83 mufkets; Second Company in blue fatigue drefs, numbering 61 mufkets; Line and Staff Officers numbering 31; total, 175 men.

Putnam Phalanx, *Major* Horace Goodwin, Commandant; Line and Staff Officers, numbering 36; Standard Bearer and Guard, 8; Privates, Firft Company, numbering 54 mufkets; Second Company, 53 mufkets; Drum Band, 10 pieces; total, 161 men.

Detachment of Marine Corps of Artillery, *Orderly Sergeant* George E. Brown, Commandant, numbering 20 men.

The line marched up Broad ftreet and down Weftminfter ftreet, through Market Square and up North Main ftreet to the Quarters of the Phalanx, at the Earl Houfe, where the latter were left by the Efcort, which was marched to the Armory and difmiffed. During the entire line of march, the ftreets were thronged with Spectators, flags were difplayed from various points, and the enthufiafm was intenfe. A prominent Journal of Providence fays, that "the Reception and Parade formed one of the moft brilliant Pageants ever witneffed in our City." In the afternoon the Phalanx marched to the Armory of the Marine Artillery and depofited their mufkets. The time, till evening, was paffed in interchange of courtefies, many diftinguifhed Citizens of Providence calling at the Head-Quarters to pay their refpects to the Members of the Phalanx.

THE BANQUET.

In the evening a complimentary Banquet to the Phalanx was given by the Infantry, in Pratt's Hall. The Phalanx was efcorted from their Quarters by the Light Infantry, and entered the Hall at precifely eight o'clock. The invited Guefts had previoufly affembled, and one of the ample galleries was filled with the fairer portion of Creation—an unufual compliment, as it is noted in the Journals of the day, that this was the firft time in the Hiftory of feftive Scenes of this fort in Providence, that Ladies by their prefence had graced the Gathering. The Hall was thronged. In addition to the Infantry and their immediate Guefts, the Phalanx, the Old Guard were prefent in full force and uniform, and a large number of diftinguifhed Gentlemen, among whom were His Excellency *Gov.* Turner, with members of his Staff, (His Honor *Mayor* Knight was prefent as a member of the Old Guard,) *Hon.* Albert C. Greene, ex-U. S. Senator, *Hon.* James F. Simmons, *Hon.* Thomas Davis, *Hon.* Walter R. Danforth, *Hon.* Walter S. Burges, *Hon.* John R. Bartlett, *Secretary of State*, *Hon.* Albert S. Gallup, *Rev. Dr.* Barnas Sears, Prefident of Brown Univerfity, *Rev.* C. H. Fay, *Quar. Gen.* T. J. Stead, the Officers of the Marine Corps of Artillery, *Lt. Col.* N. Van Slyck of the Providence Artillery, *Col.* C. T. Robbins of the National Cadets, *Col.* H. T. Siffon of the Mechanic Rifles, and many other Gentlemen of note and fundry Members of the Rhode Ifland Bar. No event of fimilar character in Providence has ever called together an affemblage of more diftinguifhed Individuals.

The Banquet itfelf was beyond all praife. Six long tables filled the Hall, covers were laid for four hundred and forty Perfons, and every feat was filled. An unufually magnificent difplay of flowers formed an additional attraction.

Col. W. W. Brown prefided. On his right were feated the Major Commandant and *Lieut.* Allyn, of the Phalanx; on the left, his Excellency *Gov.* Turner of Rhode Ifland, and *Mayor* Knight of Providence. A bleffing was pronounced by the *Rev.* C. H. Fay, and after an hour devoted to the fubftantials fpread before them, *Col.* Brown called the audience to order and briefly remarked as follows:

<blockquote>
I am aware my pofition is fuch that our ftranger Friends moft naturally turn their eyes towards me, expecting a fpeech; but my Comrades and Fellow-citizens do not expect it. * * My Command, many years ago, very fortunately, paffed a vote empowering me, under all circumftances and on any Occafion, to make a demand upon any Member. I therefore call upon my Commiffary, Rodman.
</blockquote>

Commiffary Rodman refponded to the call of his veteran Commander, and welcomed the Guefts of the Corps in the following eloquent manner:

The Welcome.

Mr. Commandant, Officers and Privates of the Putnam Phalanx:—
The annals of Rhode Ifland commence with the word "What-Cheer," the word of Welcome which fell upon the ear of him who firft planted his foot within her Borders.

It is our Rhode Ifland word of Greeting and our municipal Watch-Word; and I affure you, Gentlemen, that the air never more joyoufly vibrated to its utterance than at this moment, while in behalf of our Commandant, and thefe my Brethren of the Firft Light Infantry, I fay to you each and all, "What-Cheer."

In thus welcoming you, the path opens moft alluringly to indulge the affociations which the Occafion fo naturally awakens. Who can look upon your uniform and not feel the Patriotic and the emotional kindling and rifing within his breaft?

Memories come thronging thick and faft of all the Heroic ftruggles of the Revolutionary Conteft and thofe which anteceded it. I now fee in the darknefs of Colonial Night your heroic Putnam chained and helplefs between contending Hofts, the bullets hurtling around him like a leaden ftorm. I fee the flames kindling around him at the ftake, and hear the Indian's wild yell of fiendlike revenge. I fee him at Bunker Hill with our own gallant Greene. Ay, Gentlemen, the whole Panorama of Freedom's ftruggle paffes in quick review before me as I look upon your honored coftume. When thefe fcenes are awakened (and they cannot be too often) how deeply fhould the Fountains of our Gratitude be ftirred, and how earneftly fhould our Patriotifm be anew enkindled. General Putnam was yours—General Greene was ours, and both were Wafhington's, and Wafhington and all by whom he was furrounded were Freedom's, and all of Freedom's then, is ours by inheritance now.

They mingled their powers and fympathies, and in concert reared the Altar of Liberty, and cemented with their valor the arches of its Holy Temple, and ever through its length and breadth fhould roll, full-toned and ftrong, one ceafelefs Anthem of united and grateful Praife.

But I fee before me the honored Chief Magiftrate of our little State, and I muft not invade his prerogative—His honor the Mayor of our city, who will rightly claim the grateful privilege of welcoming you in behalf of his Fellow-citizens—and it only remains for me in the name of the Firft Light Infantry, to extend to you a Soldier's Welcome—Welcome in the name of a Soldier's Brotherhood—Welcome as the Sons of one of the Old Thirteen—Welcome in the name of mingled Revolutionary memories—Welcome as Reprefentatives of one of the pureft of Commonwealths—Welcome in the bonds of loved and cherifhed memories of your beautiful City—Welcome as

Statesmen, Soldiers, Citizens, Men—Sons of the Land of Roger Sherman, to the City of Roger Williams.

>We rouſe the drum with jocund roll,
>While ſoul reſponſive beats to ſoul,
>And makes theſe walls with echoes ring,
>As now with heart and voice we ſing,
>>What-Cheer.

>Swell the clarion loud and long,
>Wake the harp to frolic ſong,
>Let the cymbals claſhing meet,
>While as one we now repeat,
>>What-Cheer.

>Gem with deathleſs light the hours,
>Garland them with fadeleſs flowers,
>That in time's far diſtant night,
>They may gleam with holy light,
>Round the path of each and all
>Now within this feſtive hall.

Muſic—"Hail to the Chief."

The Major Commandant of the Phalanx called upon *Lieut.* T. M. Allyn, *Mayor* of Hartford, to reſpond.

Speech of Lieut. Allyn.

Colonel Commandant, Officers and Soldiers of the First Light Infantry Company:—I was about to ſay, that it has ſeldom fallen to my lot to perform a more pleaſing ſervice, than has been aſſigned to me on this Occaſion; but after the eloquent introduction to which we have juſt liſtened, I am almoſt induced to indulge a different thought upon that ſubject.

As a repreſentative of the City of Hartford and as a member of the Putnam Phalanx, I ſeize this opportunity to tender to you our heartfelt Acknowledgments, at the kind and warm Reception you have given us to-day.

The relation between Civil and Military inſtitutions has, I think, been miſconceived in ſome meaſure. They are more neceſſary to each other than has been generally imagined. I am aware, Sir, that where the great maſs of a Community acts upon the ſtrict principles of Juſtice and Equity—that great divine principle of "doing unto others as you would they ſhould do to you," there is no need, perhaps, of Civil Government, nor of Military Organizations, to aſſiſt and ſupport it; but ſuch an Organization is not ours, and we live not under ſo perfect and harmonious a ſyſtem of humanity as that. What is Civil Government? What enforces its laws? Is there any Power in the mere enactment of thoſe laws? No; we muſt look back of that, and there we ſee the firſt Military Organization of our Country.

I might go further, and ſay that without this Power to render certain and ſuſtain the execution of laws, Civil Government would be "as ſounding braſs and a tinkling cymbal"—a mere rope of ſand to be ſwept away in the firſt turmoil of riot within our borders, or upon the firſt inſurrection or rebellion within our Land.

To this arm we muſt look as the great Support of Civil Government in ſecuring the perpetuity of our beloved and cheriſhed Inſtitutions.

This Battalion, Sir, which bears the honored name of one of the diſtinguiſhed Heroes of the Revolution, is now returning from a battlefield of that great ſtruggle no leſs diſtinguiſhed than the heights of Bunker Hill; where the troops of Connecticut, New Hampſhire and Maſſachuſetts, met ſhoulder to ſhoulder, fought and bled and died —too many of them!—to emancipate three millions of people from the Colonial deſpotiſm of the Britiſh Empire, and to uſher into exiſtence the Nation which now extends over the vaſt plains of Independent America.

The moſt ſanguine of thoſe Heroes could hardly have anticipated the marvellous progreſs which we—knowing then little of manufactures and the mechanic arts, with a commerce monopolized by the Mother country—have already made, and it needs no prophetic inſpiration to foretell the ſpread of our Inſtitutions over the entire Continent of North America.

As I beheld the Stars and Stripes floating aloft on entering your beautiful City, I felt within my boſom a ſpirit of patriotic Pride in reflecting upon the rapid communication which enables us to paſs in a ſingle day through ſeveral of theſe independent Sovereignties, while at the ſame time I was a Citizen of the United States and entitled to all the rights and privileges of a Citizen of any State; and I truſt no future generation will be allowed to look upon that Flag with a ſingle Star or Stripe obliterated.

Our Country of to-day is the Country which the wifdom and forefight of our Fathers have made for us. It ftill claims at our hands, and I truft it will always receive, our warmeft Affections and our continued Support.

Mufic—NATIONAL AIR.

Col. Brown arofe and announced that *Affiftant Commiffary* Thomas A. Doyle had been appointed to act as Toaft Mafter of the occafion. In accepting the appointment, Mr. Doyle remarked as follows:

SPEECH OF ASSISTANT COMMISSARY DOYLE.

It is with a great deal of pleafure that I find myfelf enabled to render any fervice on an Occafion of this nature, which tends to bring the Citizens of different States into friendly relations with each other, and to rivet the more clofely the bonds of Brotherhood, in our common Country. The frequent interchange of focial courtefies between one State and another, and one fection and another, will tend to ftrengthen Government and greatly increafe our Love of Country. Were they far more frequent than they now are, there would be fewer demagogues and more Patriots.

Could you have been with me in the recent vifit to the great City of the Weft, and feen the men gathered from every State and Territory in our Union, from the Atlantic to the Pacific, from the St. Lawrence to the Gulf of Mexico; could you have beheld the meetings, as if from the fame State and almoft from the fame Town, you would never fear that a fingle Star or Stripe would ever be ftricken from our National Emblem.

But it is not for me to fpeak on this occafion; I am only to call upon others. Permit me to fay, however, in paffing, that the Infantry Company claims among its members fome of our moft diftinguifhed men. The reprefentative of our City government, his Honor the Mayor, prefent on this occafion, is a member of the Infantry. We alfo claim the Speaker of the Houfe of Reprefentatives, the Secretary of State, and with pride we point to his Excellency, our prefent Governor.

I give you, as the firft regular toaft—

The State of Rhode Ifland—One of the Old Thirteen, who with her veteran fifter, Connecticut, did battle for the Liberty we enjoy.

Mufic—"OLD BRISTOL."

His Excellency *Gov.* Turner, of Rhode Ifland, rofe and refponded as follows:

SPEECH OF GOVERNOR TURNER.

Colonel Commandant:—My thanks are due for being permitted to add a word of Welcome on this Occafion, and allow me to fay, at the outfet, that I am proud of being enrolled as a member of the Firft Light Infantry Company.

By virtue of my office, I am Commander-in-chief of the Militia of this State. It is fitting that I fhould participate in a feftive Occafion like the prefent, and it gives me great pleafure on this evening to meet and welcome fo many of the diftinguifhed Sons of Connecticut, and that pleafure is greatly increafed from the fact that for the firft time I behold the prefence of Ladies to lend a charm to our feftivities. I could wifh that the capacity of this fpacious Hall were doubled, that room might be made for them at the tables by our fides.

Gentlemen of the Putnam Phalanx—I feel fure that I exprefs the fentiments of all my Conftituents, when I, as their reprefentative and as Commander-in-Chief of the Military of Rhode Ifland, welcome you, as I now do, to our little State.

It is a fource of great gratification to me, as it is to all Lovers of their Country to witnefs the kindly feelings that exift between the Citizens of the feveral States of this Union. This mutual good feeling fhould be cherifhed and encouraged by every honeft, laudable means, and I know of no way more effectual than by fuch Gatherings as the prefent.

In welcoming you to Rhode Ifland I feel that we are honored by fuch a vifit from our friends, the Military of a fifter State, and in welcoming an Organization like that before me, which fo nobly reprefents the Military of Connecticut. We bid you a hearty Welcome to all that we have that will add to the real enjoyment of your vifit to our City.

I had an opportunity, Gentlemen, on a recent occafion, in company with the Firft Light Infantry, on their vifit to Connecticut, to witnefs and partake of the hofpitalities of His Excellency Governor Buckingham, and I am difappointed at not feeing him on this Occafion; his prefence would have added ftill more to the pleafure of our meeting.

There is a Gentleman prefent who is too modeft, I underftand, to fpeak in praife of his own State, but would accept the privilege of fpeaking for Rhode Ifland. I will give you as a fentiment, and call upon the Hon. I. W. Stuart, of Hartford, to refpond to that portion of it:

The Volunteer Militia of Connecticut and Rhode Ifland—They are not only good Soldiers, but an honor to their native States.

Hon. I. W. Stuart, *Judge Advocate* of the Putnam Phalanx, refponded as follows:

Speech of Judge Advocate Stuart.

Colonel Commandant, and Officers and Soldiers of the First Light Infantry Company:—Were I to exprefs the predominating fatisfaction in my own mind juft at this moment, I fhould fay it lies in the fact that I am here, with the Putnam Phalanx, from old Connecticut, participating in the good old State of Rhode Ifland, in a Feftivity which fills the body with repaft, the Mind with thoughtfulnefs, and the Hearts of the Putnam Phalanx, I am fure, with thankfulnefs for the courtefy and bounty of the Providence Firft Light Infantry. You have indeed made us at home here, Colonel Brown, and with fuch prodigal and cordial Hofpitality for a ftimulant as this with which our Battalion is now furrounded, I fhall take very great pleafure, I affure you, in refponding to the toaft to your State.

Connecticut and Rhode Ifland, Sir, took out their Charters of Government—thofe fubftantial ones which they received from Charles the Second—at very nearly one and the fame time. They enjoyed under them the fame Powers, the fame Privileges, the fame Immunities. They alone, of all the Old Thirteen Colonies, could point to them as to the Parchments of true Freedom; and fpite of the collifion occafioned for a while by their claufes relating to territory—fpite of the temporary ufurpations of the tyrannizing Sir Edmond Andros—and in defiance of all the infidious attacks of enemies to the Colonies, of Britifh Parliaments, and of the Crown,—Connecticut and Rhode Ifland, fide by fide, and fhoulder to fhoulder—we, for One hundred and fifty-fix years, you here, your Excellency, for One hundred and feventy-nine, I think,—lived, loved, and glorioufly profpered under thefe Sovereign Grants; grants which continued to form the Conftitutions of our refpective States for a period long fubfequent to the Revolution.

It is with an efpecial fympathy, therefore, of pleafure and of pride, that the citizens of Connecticut look upon Rhode Ifland, when the curtain is lifted from her Paft—as, gratefully to myfelf, I am called upon to lift it now, and to reveal fome of the Monuments which, under her old Charter, fhe has erected to Liberty and to God.

Far back—even in your infancy as a State—we behold your People, even when they were fighting the wildernefs, a profperous Community. But eighteen years only after your illuftrious Roger Williams, with Harris and Smith, and Verin, and Angell, and Wickes, his five companions, firft in a fingle canoe croffed the Seekonk, to found this your City of Providence, we find your People, as in their own recorded language they fay, drinking "of the cup of as great Liberties" as any that they could hear of "under the whole Heaven"; and fo exempt from the burden of public charges, they add, as even "not to know what an Excife meant," and to have "almoft forgotten what Tithes—yea, or Taxes—were, either to Church or Commonwealth." To this effect, gentlemen, your own town of Providence officially reports, through Gregory Dexter, its Clerk, in a letter addreffed to Sir Henry Vane, in the gray Year of fixteen hundred and fifty-four!

And down from this early period, down upon the ftream of Time as Rhode Ifland moves, we find a praifeworthy progrefs in her Laws, her Inftitutions, her Education, her Induftry, and her Arts. With her power inextricably lodged in the hands of her People—with her Spirit, in general, high-toned by Good Morals and Religion—with her Labor enterprifing, ambitious, inventive, and accumulative—the Anchor for her feal, and Hope for her motto—fhe has fteadily advanced in a career of profperity whofe Fruits at the prefent moment —whofe coveted fruits of Health, Wealth, and Content—are plucked, proportionably to her territorial extent, by as many happy hands as anywhere upon the face of the American Continent are ftretched out for human Bleffings.

As we come down to the Revolutionary period—that with which the Putnam Phalanx is more immediately concerned—our intereft in your Hiftory becomes deepened. For here, emphatically, and in closer Union than any other States among the Old Thirteen—save Massachusetts—Rhode Island and Connecticut played conspicuous parts, and it is with uncommon satisfaction, therefore, that we of this Phalanx recall the manner in which Rhode Island performed her Role.

The spirited opposition of your People, ere the Revolution broke out, to the odious Revenue acts of Great Britain—your special and frequent Town Assemblies, particularly here in Providence, in which you boldly denounced these acts as encroachments, all of them, on the incontestible Rights of "his Majesty's liege subjects" everywhere; your Resolutions, far back as August, 1765, in which, with a directness and daring hardly surpassed even by those immortal Resolves of Patrick Henry's, on the same subject, in the land of the Old Dominion, you declared against the public grievances, and pointed to Independence; the Illuminations, and *feu de joies*, and Toasts, and Speeches, and other thousand rejoicings, with which you celebrated the repeal of the hated Stamp Act, and in 1768, formally dedicated your Tree of Liberty; the Oath your people took beneath that tree, "in the name and behalf," as was their language upon the occasion, "in the name and behalf of all the true Sons of Liberty in America, Great Britain, Ireland, Corsica, or wheresoever they may be dispersed throughout the world," to support and maintain the Freedom which "our renowned Forefathers fought out and found under trees, and in the wilderness"—all these your Acts and Pledges in behalf of Liberty which preceded the outbreak of the Revolution, this Phalanx dwells upon with heartfelt pride.

With pride also we gaze, through the glass of History, upon your little Squadron of long boats, eight in number, and crowded with a band of your daring Shipmasters and Merchants, as, in the Spring of 1772, under the command of your intrepid Whipple, they carried that Oath of Rhode Island resistance to which I have referred into startling effect, and burned the offensive Gaspee to the water's edge. There—in that exploit down upon Namquit Point—we of this Phalanx hail the *first* open and armed opposition upon the American Continent of the American Colonies, to the King of England's martial power. For there, just at that moment when Ruddington, the Commander of the Gaspee, discharged at the approaching Party the pistols which he held, and in return was wounded by a musket ball in the left groin, there was shed, in fact, the *first blood* of the American

Revolution. A Providence man it was who fired the firſt defenſive Gun in this great Conteſt, and at a Company of Providence men it was that the firſt Britiſh ball was diſcharged. Men of Rhode Iſland, you wear the Laurel from this ſource, to your glory, and forever!

Again, gentlemen, we follow you with lively joy, in March, 1775, to the public Market-place in this your City of Providence, and there behold your People kindle a craving fire, and at the time when Tea was made the vehicle of a moſt unconſtitutional tax, burn up the obnoxious ſhrub—the Free-will Offering, moſt of it, of your patriotic Ladies; Aye, Ladies, [ſaid the ſpeaker, addreſſing the numerous Fair Ones who graced the Gallery of the Hall,] claim the force of this patriotic faԑt all to yourſelves. And, Gentlemen, we ſee your People juſt at this moment of the conflagration, add to its fuel the hoſtile Speech of the Prime Miniſter of England, Lord North's; and the Tory journals of Rivington, and Mills, and Hicks—while one of your ſpirited Sons of Liberty, lampblack and bruſh in hand, perambulated your ſtreets, unpainting and obliterating the word *Tea* from all the ſhop ſigns of your Town—and not one Soul within your borders was found "poor enough to do reverence" as a mourner at this your funeral of Madame Souchong.

We gaze, too, with pride upon your full One thouſand men, who rouſed by the Lexington Alarm, paraded at once here in your City, for a quick march to the ſcene of ſtrife—while the flaming Beacon from your Eaſt Hill, told to Newport, and your whole ſurrounding country even to Proſpeԑt Hill in Cambridge, and to our own New London and Norwich, and diſtant Pomfret, the fierce alarms of War—

> "Like an exhaled meteor,
> Blazing forth the portents of broached miſchief
> To the times."

It was the fortune of War, Gentlemen of Rhode Iſland, in that great Struggle which made us free, as is familiar hiſtory, that Newport, and the Iſland upon which it reſts, for upwards of three years, ſhould remain in the poſſeſſion of the enemy. Now, gentlemen, the Putnam Phalanx recalls with deep intereſt the faԑt, that when in December, 1776, that huge Britiſh fleet, with four thouſand troops under Sir Henry Clinton, puſhed up Narraganſett Bay and ſeized your beautiful Newport, and fearfully menaced the whole adjacent country—Conneԑticut—inſtantaneouſly rouſed to aԑtion by her patriotic Governor Trumbull—not only ſent you her Dyer, and Law, and Wales, and

Hofmer, here at Providence, in union with Committees from all the New England States, to concert meafures "for mutual and immediate defence and fafety"—but fent you alfo Ten hundred and ninety-two of her Soldier-fons, together with a gallant Troop of Light Horfe under her brave Major Ebenezer Backus, and an abundance of military ftores—here in conjunction with your own Troops—your "Independent Companies" of Providence particularly, and your Artillery, under the ever active Col. Daniel Tillinghaft—here gallantly to ftrive againft the appalling Invafion.

And we recall alfo with intereft the fact, that when in 1778, upon a frefh Enterprife to expel the Enemy from Newport, Sullivan, then in chief command, fent to Connecticut for more Troops, again our Governor—in addition to Seven hundred and twenty-eight men from our State already then quartered with you—fpeedily fent you on Seven companies more, together with numerous Volunteers, one hundred barrels of powder, and other copious ftores—once again with the brave Soldiery of Rhode Ifland to co-operate againft the Foe.

And pleafantly alfo we recall the fact, that in 1779, Connecticut furnifhed yet another large Quota of Troops to the Rhode Ifland defence. And what is more—and is ftrikingly expreffive of her fympathy for your People—when the long prefence of the Foe had cut off your Trade here, and your Navigation and Fifhery, and debarred many of your Citizens from cultivating their lands, and a famine, in confequence, ftared them in the face, Connecticut promptly fent you relief in food—fent you feven thoufand bufhels of grain—fent you money—collecting her contributions through a warrant in favor of your Jonathan Otis and Oliver K. Warner of Newport, which, by Governor Trumbull himfelf, was addreffed to every Religious Society in our State, and was met by a hearty and humane refponfe.

And when, in 1780, another moft formidable Britifh fleet menaced Newport—in refponfe to the preffing folicitations of Gen. Heath and your own Governor Greene, Connecticut again quickly fent you aid. She fent you half the men from her four eaftern Brigades—her Troop of Veterans from Canterbury under Capt. Timothy Backus, and her Company of Matroffes from Pomfret under Captain Daniel Tyler—once more, in warm concert with Rhode Ifland and Continental Troops, to labor for the expulfion of the Foe.

And when, through the extraordinary and precipitate abandonment by the Foe of Newport, the pall of Britifh power, to the univerfal

Joy, was at laft, Gentlemen, lifted from your beautiful feaboard, no State in the Union, more than Connecticut, let me affure you, was gladdened by the refult. Long and unflinchingly had you here of Rhode Ifland ftriven to accomplifh this triumphant refult; and at laft you rejoiced in it. In defiance of dangers which, much of the time, ftared you in the face more imminently than they did moft other States, you devoted your blood and your treafure to the Revolutionary ftruggle — day after day and year after year — with a Spirit that never quailed, and an Energy that never faltered. This you did, not only upon the land, but alfo upon the ftormy feas — upon which your gallant Cruifers, like the *Hawk* under your immortal SILAS TALBUT, achieved many confpicuous triumphs; and upon which it is your juft boaft, that in Auguft, 1775, through inftructions from your General Affembly to your Delegates then in Congrefs, you made the firft movement in the American States for the eftablifhment of a Continental Navy, and gave to this Navy, when it was founded, in Commodore EZEK HOPKINS, its firft Commander-in-chief.

Juftly, then, Sir, does the Battalion which I have the honor now to reprefent, warm with fuch military Memories as thefe to which I allude, and to the Prowefs of Rhode Ifland, render the tribute of its patriotic refpect. Organized as we are, as I have already fuggefted, for the efpecial purpofe of renewing and ftimulating thofe thoughts and affociations which clufter around the glorious War for American Independence, our hearts, Gentlemen, let me affure you, beat high when we find, that to our own Connecticut treafure-houfe of the Revolutionary Paft, we can add a ftore of Memories fo rich and varied, and patriotic, as thofe which fpring up here among the beautiful Ifles and along the hiftoric Headlands of fair Narraganfett Bay.

Your Governor Greene, the perfonal Friend, and intimate military Coadjutor of our own immortal "Rebel" Governor Trumbull — your Brigadier General Greene, next to Wafhington probably the moft accomplifhed Officer in the American fervice of the Revolution — your Ezek Hopkins, the firft Commodore, as I have faid, of our Continental Navy, and the victor at Naffau — your heroic Commodore Whipple, and Major Talbut, and Colonel Tillinghaft, and Colonel Olney — your John Brown, that eminently bold and ceafeleflly enterprifing lover of Liberty, who, chiefly, I believe, contrived the conflagration of the Gafpee — your John Updike, David Howell, William Rhodes, Paul Allen, Jonathan Arnold, William Earle, Ambrofe Page, Theodore Foster, William Ruffell, Nicholas Cooke, Joseph Brown, Jabez Bowen, and others your leading Patriots and gallant men—all, both on the Land, and on the Sea, whom you gave to the counsels, and with whom you recruited the Battalions of the Continent—these are all the pride of the Putnam Phalanx, as well as your own—the pride also of Connecticut—the pride, too, of our whole Country. We claim a share in the renown of them all. Their patriotic Virtues, their disinterestedness, their zeal, their sublime endurance, their joys, their sorrows, their reverses, their triumphs—we also lay title to these as part and parcel, interwoven, indissolubly interwoven with our great National Heritage of Freedom.

Happy, Gentlemen, the lot of Rhode Island to have participated so reputably as she did in the Revolutionary Struggle! Happy, particularly, the fortune of Providence to have been, as she was, one among the Leaders in our midst—one among the foremost in that great and good Work, which, not only within her own captivating borders, but elsewhere from sea to sea, over a gigantic Continent, has spread the munificent and imperishable sunshine of Liberty.

In conclusion, Gentlemen, allow me to propose a sentiment:

Rhode Island and Connecticut—Connecticut and Rhode Island—Twin nurses, ever vigorous, of Colonial and Revolutionary Freedom. May their patriotic History be written forever in the hearts of the American People!

Second regular toast—

The State of Connecticut—The Mother of a numerous and distinguished progeny of Heroes. The memory of the noblest of them all is perpetuated in the Putnam Phalanx.

Col. Irish, of *Gov.* Buckingham's Staff, was called upon to respond, which he did by a summons upon *Hon.* H. C. Deming, of Hartford, who spoke as follows:

Speech of Assistant Commissary Deming.

Colonel Commandant and Gentlemen:—I supposed that my friend from New London was too much of a Soldier, and also too much of an Orator, to call upon a Soldier to play the part of an Orator; more especially, a heavy Infantry Soldier, exhausted by an arduous Campaign.

There are certain Occupations which, when united in the same Individual, are congenial and harmonious, and certain other Occupations, Professions and Trades which, when united in the same Individual, are uncongenial and inharmonious. The profession of Preacher and Lecturer is of the former class, for he can lecture his sermons and preach his lectures; so of the Banker and Broker, for the Broker can shave notes with the bills which the Banker manufactures by the wholesale; the butcher and boarding-house keeper have certain affinities, for the boarding-house keeper can use the unsaleable joints of the butcher. I have heard it intimated too, that the dog-fancier and sausage-maker may be profitably united in the same individual, and some malignant cynic has asserted, (I hope the Surgeons of the different Battalions will pardon me for repeating the scandal,) that the Doctor and Undertaker should always be united.

The most uncongenial and inharmonious blending, however, which in my experience I ever discovered in the same Individual, is that of Soldier and Orator—particularly if you chance to be a Soldier in a heavy Infantry Company.

The Orator must think; but what chance is there of thinking when the small modicum of mind with which you are endowed is altogether engrossed in attempting to keep step, or in catching it after it is lost—a manœuvre consummately perplexing to me.—The Orator must have breath, but what breath is left in a heavy Infantry Orator after a five miles march. "Action, action, action," we are told by the chief of Orators, the Orator must have, but what action is left in a "Ph'lanx" Orator after these long marches and countermarches, and the taking of Boston and Charlestown by storm. Were I here as an Orator, I should attempt (though I presume unsuccessfully,) to do my *devoir* as an Orator; but I *am* here as a Soldier, and wish to be judged by you, Mr. Governor, and Colonel Commandant, by the perfection of my equipments and the precision of my drill.

For these reasons, my friend of Gov. Buckingham's Staff must not expect to shove off his appropriate Duties on to my worn-out martial energies. I supposed he was too correct a Soldier to attempt it; it is not according to the Steuben drill, nor has such an attempt been made since the "Ph'lanx" was an Institution.

My friend from New London has also called upon the *Hon.* Henry C. Deming to respond to this toast—an error into which I hardly expected so exact a Tactician would fall. We have no such handles to our names in the Military. If there is anybody with that rather uncommon prefix, he ought to be at home attending to his bufinefs, and not trooping round the Country in regimentals. It is the Affiftant Commiffary of the Putnam Phalanx that you fee before you—Lieut. Henry C. Deming.

Providence muft either be one of the moft agreeable places in the World, or I chance to light upon it in its happieft moods, and to meet all its pleafanteft People. The afpect of things about the Depot impreffes the ftranger favorably. The Area there is fpacious, and was to-day certainly fufficient *airy;* the Streets are all wide and well paved, the gutters bridged at the croffwalks with thefe neat and convenient iron coverings; the Pavements are broad and fmooth, and clean and well curbed;—I call upon our Superintendent of Streets to make note of this. The Houfes have a comfortable look, and the whole City the appearance of a permanent dwelling place inftead of a temporary encampment. The Ladies are all handfome, and fend handfome bouquets to eloquent Judge Advocates. The Men are all hofpitable: one hurries you off to his houfe, and before you have fairly picked your teeth another gathers you into his. Your Inftitutions of Learning, of Humanity and Philanthropy, your Colleges, your Libraries, your Military Companies, particularly the Firft Light Infantry Company and your Old Veteran Guard—your fteam fire engines, your palaces of induftry, filled to overflowing with life, and dextrous and femi-vitalized machinery; your men too—your Browns, Greenes, Anthonys, Waylands, Sears—everything I fee around me in this beautiful City is fuch as to fill the meafure of the grandeft municipal Ambition.

But it is not thefe fuperficial Beauties which turn the thoughtful traveller and the ftudent of human progrefs to Providence. Here was the Birth-place and Cradle of one of the greateft reforms in opinion and practice that ever fhowered benediction on the human race. Why, Sir, this round World of ours was old and hoary and feared with crime, before it was difcovered that Opinion and Confcience fhould be free. And where was Toleration firft born and firft practiced? Not in the Mafter States of Antiquity. Not amid the fchools and groves of Athens; witnefs the firft great Mafter of intellectual Freedom taking the poifoned cup from the weeping Jailor! Not in Rome; for the whole Hiftory of ancient and modern Rome is one of Perfecution. Not in France, before or after the Baftile, nor in England before or fince the Reformation. It was not brought to this new Hemifphere by thofe who perfecuted Quakers and banifhed Baptifts. Here it was born, here in your City of Providence: and here, I pray, it may be forever moft religioufly protected.

But the fentiment to which Col. Irifh—a Soldier off duty, and a *light* Infantry one alfo—fhould have refponded, calls me to Connecticut. If I could amend the fentiment fo that it fhould read—"The State of Connecticut—The Mother of a numerous and diftinguifhed progeny, fome of the *hugeft* of whom are to be found in the Putnam Phalanx," I could prove the propofition, demonftratively, upon the fpot. I would make *profert* of our Standard-bearer, and "reft." But ferioufly, I have nothing new to tell little Rhody, our neareft neighbor, of any of our Heroes, moral or military. Of Putnam, too, the merely feftive nature of this Occafion permits me to fay but a word.

If Connecticut had forefeen her Future from 1745 to the Revolutionary period, and made for herfelf a Hero, fhe would have forever forfeited her repute for practical common-fenfe, if fhe had not made precifely fuch an one as Ifrael Putnam. The ftyle of Hero which thofe Thirty Years demanded, was effentially military, for Wars and Convulfions decifive of our Deftiny were diftinctly prognofticated, and yet a military Hero that was adapted to our peculiar wants, graded to our fcale, and willing to make himfelf generally ufeful. We were a feeble Folk, far away in the backwoods, juft opening a ftingy foil to tillage, juft beginning to raife Crops enough for Home confumption, with naught but homefpun manufactures, with the meagereft foreign Commerce, in wholefome fear of Indian maffacre—for in 1746 the tomahawk and fcalping-knife had been freely ufed within a few hours' march of our Borders—environed with French fettlements and pofts, and at times in imminent danger of vaffalage to the houfe of Bourbon, and liable to requifitions from our own Sovereign Liege whenever the Wars of European ambition kindled into flames his American Dominions. What this little frugal Colony, with its narrow theatre and diminutive operations, could have done with a Hero of more magnificent and coloffal proportions—an Alexander, a Cromwell, a Napoleon—except to offer itfelf up as one meal to his infatiate maw, it is impoffible to conceive. We craved a Hero of dauntlefs pluck, of unwearifome endurance, fhrewd, generous, felf-abnegating, fertile in expedients, with more Genius for foreft Warfare than for pitched Battles and complicated Campaigns—a Man of muscle and might and will, capable of intense wrath and invincible obstinacy, who could bend or break into military subordination and trustful self-surrender, the Connecticut levies, raw, verdant, awkward as Soldiers, but independent and self-complacent as Freeholders, while under his stubborn and imperious rule they were marched to Ticonderoga, or Frontenac, or Havana, or wherever else His Majesty chose to order them; and, after the Campaign was over and the Troops discharged, could render an exact and conscionable account of receipts and disbursements to the Commissioners of the Pay Table. We wanted a Hero shaped more like a Cincinnatus than a Cæsar, who in the breathing times of Peace, could join his Fellow-citizens in productive industry, and support the Gospel, and sit in the General Assembly, no useless drone in our hive, no barnacle on our poor treasury—a Hero who, in the fullness of time, when petitions, prayers and remonstrances had all failed, and our Inborn Rights and Privileges were brought to the arbitrament of the Battle-field, held in himself a sufficient volume of slumbering Courage and martial Enthusiasm to electrify our whole People, and dared to lead a sturdy Yeomanry where any dared to follow. The Model Man whom our Era and Environments craved was none of your imperial Spirits who bend all Mankind into homage and contemn the civil power and cross Rubicons, and convulse the World, but a Shield and Sword to an infant Commonwealth in a steady struggle with untamed Nature, and with savage and civilized Foes, the Farmer that could subdue the stubbornest glebe, the Hunter that could cope with its most formidable beasts of prey, the Ranger that could banish the terror of the Indian, and give security to the Traveller in the forest, the Laborer in the field, and the Child in the cradle, the advanced Guard on the Canadian war path, behind whom the Women and the Children could sleep secure, the trusted Leader who could hold our untried Plowmen to a breastwork of hay through three assaults from British Grenadiers.

It has always seemed to me that the ante-Revolutionary services of Putnam, in many respects most remarkable, have been dimmed by the more familiar glare of his Revolutionary exploits. The importance of the first of these Wars, in evolving the destiny of Humanity on this Continent, has also been obscured by the more palpable significance of what we call, *par excellence*, the War of Independence. They were both wars of independence—the one of independence from the Gallic race and the reactionary influences of cotemporary Gallic civilization; the other, of independence from the fetters which the narrow bigotry of the Englifh Colonial Syftem impofed upon Commerce, Manufactures and Trade, and alfo, from the Parliamentary ufurpations of our Motherland. In that minute fegment of time that feparates the Peace of '63 from the Battle of Lexington, the whole future of the Weftern Hemifphere lay "like unborn forefts in an acorn cup." In that old War which expelled from this Continent the French, and the feudal barbarities they were planting here, no Regular, not even Wolfe, no Provincial not excepting Wafhington, played a more confpicuous and impofing part than Ifrael Putnam. Had he lived in the early days of Greece and Rome when human knowledge was tranfmitted by tradition, he would have been regarded, fo Herculean were his warlike labors, as a Myth, a Child rather of Fable than of Hiftory. He plunged with Williams of Williamftown into the bloody defile where that dauntlefs Philanthropift fell; he ftruggled with Lyman for his dearly bought victory over Diefkau; he received the dying Lord Howe in his arms before the fatal breaft work of Ticonderoga; he marched with Bradfteet to Prefque Ifle, and when Spain became a party to the ftrife, he ferved under Albermarle in the Weft Indies, and fcratched from the crevices of the rocky foil the earth on which the Siege Artillery was planted that thundered againft Havana. He marched with Amherft to Montreal by the roundabout way of the New York wildernefs, lake Ontario and the river St. Lawrence. What would the Phalanx fay to a march like that!

The part of this large field, thus haftily fketched in outline, which Putnam moft bountifully filled in with his peculiar and characteriftic Audacity, was that region of unfurpaffed natural beauty where, on the fide of France, Ticonderoga and Crown Point, and on that of England, Fort William Henry and Edward, ftand as fentinels at the gateway of the Canadas, and Lake George and the head-waters of the Hudfon lie in the embrace of mountains. Take a point at the foot of Lake George, and fweep round it a circle with fome ten or twelve miles radius, and you will fcarcely find a fquare foot of earth that has not been preffed by the foot, nor a reach of water that has not been cut by the oar of old Put.

Thefe and his Revolutionary fervices conftitute his claim upon the everlafting Gratitude of that Colony to which he was the military right Arm for more than twenty-five years. And what has our Colony done to reward fuch fervices? Built a fmall box of granite over his Remains and covered it with a cheap ftone now broken and defaced. The greateft Pride of my connection with this Putnam Phalanx is not in the Military laurels it has juft won, but in my knowledge that the Determination is living and burning in the breaft of many of its Members, to build over thefe Immortal Afhes, a Monument, not altogether incommenfurate with our obligations, not altogether unworthy his world-wide Fame.

Third regular toaft—

The Senate of the United States—May Dignity and Integrity ever characterize the Councils of this, one of the moft influential Political Bodies in the World.

Mufic—"STAR-SPANGLED BANNER."

Refponded to by *Hon.* James F. Simmons, of the United States Senate.

Fourth regular toaft—

The City of Providence—Her Workfhops, her Factories, and her Warehoufes afford the beft Evidence of her Profperity.

Mufic—"TWILIGHT DEWS."

His Honor Jabez B. Knight, *Mayor* of Providence, refponded to the above fentiment.

MAYOR KNIGHT'S ADDRESS.

Mr. Commander:—I am very glad of this opportunity to extend to your Guefts upon this Occafion, the Officers and Members of the Putnam Phalanx, a cordial Welcome to our City, and in behalf of my Fellow-citizens to exprefs the pleafure which their prefence here gives us all.

Gentlemen, we have often heard of your Affociation, and of your efficiency and difcipline as a Military Body, and as the Chief Magistrate of our City, I offer you fuch Hofpitalities and Attention as we can beftow. Our Citizens have looked forward to this Day with more than ordinary intereft, and I fpeak the general feeling when I tell you they are highly gratified, not only with feeing you here, but pleafed to do all in their power to make your vifit pleafant and agreeable. We are honored by your prefence, Gentlemen, and we wifh you to feel at home among us, and truft you will enjoy your vifit here. We are honored with the prefence of the Chief Magiftrate of your City, His Honor Mayor Allyn; to him I would extend a heartfelt and an earneft Welcome to our City, and I beg leave to affure him that we are happy to fee him here. We had many reafons for defiring to fee you. You have among you many Gentlemen to whom we are indebted for kindneffes and attentions in times paft. The intercourfe between your City and ours, and between your Citizens and ours, fince the opening of the Railroad, has been intimate and friendly; and I defire to tender to you my congratulations upon the high pofition your City maintains, and for the Profperity and Succefs which have always attended her. Her Inftitutions are among the beft in the Land; the Induftry and Enterprife of her Citizens are not furpaffed anywhere. I truft fhe will continue to extend and increafe in ufefulnefs, and in all that pertains to her Welfare and to the Happinefs of her People. You have with you, alfo, thofe who have occupied pofitions of honor and truft in Public Affairs; Gentlemen who have made their names honored abroad and at home; whofe fervices have been of great value to their Country and to their Home. To all I bid a cordial and heartfelt Welcome.

In conclufion, permit me to exprefs the hope that the Cities of Hartford and Providence, which are bound together with Bands of Iron, may be ftill more clofely cemented by the Ties of Friendfhip, and enjoy a further and better acquaintance.

At this point of the proceedings *ex-Mayor* **Rodman** rofe and prefented to the Phalanx a fragment of the Roger Williams rock, with the following appropriate remarks:

While I fat liftening to the eloquent remarks of the Gentleman from Hartford, as he fpoke of the Memories of our Revolutionary Hiftory, the thought prefented itfelf to my mind, that the richeft of all the mental powers, is Memory. How we love to revel in its funfhine,

Gentlemen. How we joy to go back to the Hours of Childhood and to live over again its frolic and its fun, and how all along the pathway of Life, this Power cheers and enlivens the Soul. In our hours of defpondency how it awakens reflection, and we walk down through memory's Picture Gallery and by the aid of that ftrange, myfterious power of feparation, we veil the dark and gloomy, and linger long and lovingly before thofe that glow all around with the Spring-like Garlands of Affection and of Hope. Such a Picture is now prefent to my mind; and my Brothers of the Infantry well know to what I allude. I fpeak of that vifit to Hartford, a few years fince, which can never fade from our Memories fo long as the Revolutionary Memories there awakened by the fame lips which have thrilled you this Evening, are thrilling and echoing through our chambers of delightful recollection.

You well recollect, Brethren of the Infantry, that on our arrival in Hartford, the honorable Gentleman led us up to one of thofe Old Monuments of the Paft, ever prefent to our Memory by this Gift before you, (a piece of the old Charter Oak in a glafs cafe and fuitably infcribed, and prefented to the Infantry fome years fince by Mr. Stuart.) Juft before our arrival there, that old foreft Monarch had fallen to the Earth.

Our Fathers found it ftanding there, and there in obedience to the requeft of the Red Man it was permitted to ftand, for when it put forth its leaves in the Spring-time he knew it was the hour to plant the maize; and thus it ftood fecure from the vandalifm of Civilization, becaufe the Savage pleaded for it;—and for—oh how holy a purpofe was it preferved. The hand of your own Wadfworth confecrated it, when he placed beneath, and within it, that old Charter to which my Brother has fo gracefully alluded in connection with our own. It is proftrate now—but it fell like a true Hero. It fuccumbed only to Death. Storms affailed it—the Lightning madly hurtled around it; but it defied their every affault—and only by the gradual decay of Age, and beneath the corroding touch of Time, did it yield its power, and then fell full of years, clothed with all the memories of our Nation's life. Like Royalty in ruins, that old King lay before us, and to perpetuate the memory of fo illuftrious a Landmark in the pathway of our Liberty and our Progrefs, this fragment of the Charter Oak was prefented to the Firft Light Infantry, by our honored Friend.

What return can we make to the Putnam Phalanx, my Brethren,

for fuch a Gift? What can we prefent as a counterpart to it? With your permiffion, Mr. Commandant, in the name and in behalf of the Firft Light Infantry Company, I prefent you with this fragment of "Roger Williams Rock," upon which I have taken the liberty of infcribing—"This fragment of Roger Williams Rock is presented to the Putnam Phalanx, of Hartford, Conn., by the First Light Infantry Company of Providence, R. I., October 6th, 1859."

As that Charter Oak ftood upon your foil as a Memorial of our Fathers, fo, Sir, that confecrated old Rock ftill remains on the borders of our State, and that Rock, Sir, felt the firft foot-fall of the white man when he came here preaching that Liberty which not only burft the fhackles which bind the Body, but which fhould fet the Soul of man free to worfhip God, here and throughout the World, from that time forth, forever.

Hallowed as are the memories of your Charter Oak, and hallowed as the affociations are of this Pilgrim Rock, and as pleafant as it would be to indulge them now; I am admonifhed by the flying moments that I muft paufe.

More I need not fay, and Sir, fo long as the memory of that Oak lives, fo long as that Rock exifts upon the bofom of the Earth, and fo long as that fragment defies the corroding touch of Time, fo long may thefe Memories mingle and intermingle, and may they continue thus to ftrengthen the bond of Union that exifts between fellow States, until not the Stars in our Flag, but until yonder Spheres fall from the ftarry Concave, and the Sun goes out in the blacknefs of everlafting Night.

Mr. Commandant, I had purpofed fpeaking in a more playful ftrain, but the fterner prompting has ruled my utterance, and withholding, that which would make it fully appropriate, I offer you, in clofing, the following fentiment:—

> The Name and the Fame of gallant "Old Put."
> Who never would halt for an "if" or a "but,"
> But all through his Life regarded it crime,
> When the order was "march," to ever "mark time."

Mr. Stuart's Reply.

Worthy Mr. Rodman, faid the *Judge Advocate,* immediately rifing —No Gift more acceptable could have been prefented to the Putnam Phalanx than that with which you have juft now furprifed and honored us—and in behalf of the Putnam Phalanx I sincerely thank you for it. It clusters deeply interesting Associations—for in the same year in which your Roger Williams, in a little canoe—"every stroke of whose paddle removed him farther and farther from every vestige of Civilization"—crossed the Seekonk to found your City of Providence, our venerable Hooker and Haynes crossed the great River of Connecticut to found Hartford. Himself, and the first Governor of our State, were warm personal Friends. They were allied in taste— were alike benignant—were joint lovers of Liberty—and, what is especially beautiful in the lives of both, were each earnest Advocates of those great Principles of religious Toleration which have ever signally distinguished Rhode Island.

The shadow of that mighty Oak, of which this fragment before me is a memorializing specimen, was upon Hooker and Haynes and the Companions of their Emigration, when first they set up their Tabernacle in the then Wilderness of Hartford. That Rock, of which you have now so handsomely bestowed upon our Battalion a memorializing piece, received, in the then Wilderness of Providence, the first footfall of the Founder of your State. The two Specimens then, under this view, are beautifully and sublimely associated.

But the Charter Oak, Sir, is particularly memorable under another view. When, far back in the olden time, New England was suffering from a bitter Oppression—when here in your State, the usurper Andros seized your precious Charter, and broke into fragments your Colonial Seal—that Monarch Tree from which the section on your table comes—thanks to the heroic Wadsworth—saved in our State the sister-Charter to your own. It protected it until the usurpation was past—and its leaves rustled with joy, the birds sang amid its foliage, when a virtual Declaration of Independence, at the Patriotic uprising of the People in Boston and the adjacent Towns, put an end to the Tyranny of the Day.

That Declaration, good Sir, was the first of its kind that ever broke the silence of the New World. It was the noble Precursor, near two Centuries ago, of another Declaration with which Rhode Island is especially associated—and I know not how, *Commissary* Rodman, I can now better signify to you, on the part of our Major Commandant and his Battalion, our sense of the value of the Gift you have just bestowed, than by returning to you the triumphant Fact in the History of your State, that you here of Rhode Island were the first people upon the American Continent to follow up that remarkable Declaration to which I have juft referred.

Yes, Sir, by an Act of your General Affembly, in May, 1776, which is *prior* in date to that of any other of the fame Character that was paffed by any other one of the American Colonies, you here, by repealing a former Act which fecured the allegiance of Rhode Ifland to the King, virtually declared yourfelves free and independent of Britifh power. You ftruck out the King's name and Authority from all your Civil, Judicial, and Military Proceffes and Commiffions, and fubftituting in lieu thereof "the Governor and Company" of fovereign Rhode Ifland, you fuftained this your own Declaration of Independence, and the fubfequent Declaration by the United Colonies with a Courage that was untiring, and a Fidelity that never fwerved.

We of Connecticut, Sir, had long prided *ourfelves* on having given to the World the firft virtual Declaration of Independence in our Land, during the Revolutionary era, in the Inftructions to our Delegates in Congrefs which were paffed by our General Affembly on the fourteenth of *June*, 1776. That Repealing Act of yours, however, to which I have referred, paffed your General Affembly in *May* of the fame year. It preceded us — and Sir, by way of hiftoric return for the valuable gift from your Battalion, the Putnam Phalanx yields from old Connecticut to your State the honor of having been the firft among the Old Thirteen Colonies to declare herfelf free and independent of royal Sovereignty. We yield the glorious Laurel from this fource, and *place it on the brow of gallant Rhode Ifland!*

Fifth regular toaft —

The Old Guard—They unite with us in the warmeft manifeftations of Welcome to that noble body of Citizen Soldiery, the Putnam Phalanx.

Mufic—"ROAD TO BOSTON."

Geo. W. Pettes, Efq., of Bofton, was introduced by the Toaft-Mafter and refponded to the fentiment in the following effufion:

I am forry that you, Sir, fhould open on *me* fo,
For I learned, Years ago, what is *ordered* muft *be* fo —
There are many good Reafons why I fhould reject
The condition to fpeak, in the way you expect.

"Unaccuftomed in public," &c., &c.,
Of courfe, I intended, uncalled for, to go forth,
As like *all* the reft, I came only to hear,
And promptly decline when required to appear.
Befides, I've a cold, and can't talk very clearly,
And I fear the crack Speakers who follow me nearly;
And I havn't had Time, and in fine, I muft fay, Sir,
That drinking dry Toaft's not at all in my way, Sir.
   How much better 'twould be then to call up a rocket,
Who has fire in his head, and a match in his pocket;
Or to pick out fome Member who knows what he's at,
With *no* cold in his head, and no brick in his hat.
Now, though I have laid the fatirical lafh on
The mafs of apologies moft in the fafhion,
There remains the grand Reafon why I fhould be fpared
You'll pleafe to obferve, Sir, *I came unprepared.*

   I believe when he's up, the Apologift talks on
With the eafe that a Blondin a folid rope walks on,
And *this* ftyle, as well as the reft, I muft follow,
Or you may declare my Pretenfions are hollow.

   I'll tell you two ftories, to Hiftory known
With fome trifling *addenda,* but that is my own.

The royal Darius, one funfhiny day,
Drew up his Battalions in battle array
And proud of the Sight, told a veteran Greek,
Charidemus by name, of their merit to fpeak.
   And thefe are the words that the Warrior affayed—
"This Army fo vaft, fo fuperbly arrayed,
May boaft its bright Jewels, may glitter in Gold,
That the worth of habiliment cannot be told.
But it owns not the Difcipline, Honor, or Worth,
Of the fimply equipped, but courageous of Earth.
And vain are the gewgaws, and vain is the fhow
Of thofe that nor Skill nor Integrity know;
And vain to oppofe with effeminate zeal
The Phalanx of Macedon, gleaming in fteel."
   At the Court of Darius we cannot appear;
Chafidemus is duft, and no Perfians are here.

And the reign of the brave Macedonian is o'er,
But the words of the Grecian fhall live evermore.

When Xerxes advanced to Thermopylæ's ftrait,
The valiant Three Hundred advifed him to wait;
But he cared not to liften to aught that they faid,
And let twenty thoufand good Perfians be bled.
There fell the Three Hundred, but never to die
While the Sea rolls its waves, or the Stars ftud the fky.

Oh! if Colt could have furnifhed Leonidas then
With his patent Revolvers, that handful of Men
Could have built of the Perfian's long arrows and fpears
A bridge, on approved cofmopolitan piers.

I'll juft venture to fay, in a little afide,
A word of fome weight, that will tickle your Pride.
We are not informed of the width of the Pafs
That Leonidas kept, but however it was,
Though you cannot ftand in Leonidas' place,
You may happen to be in a fimilar cafe;
And in order to fave all the reft from mifhap,
You might chuck in an Enfign to fill up the gap.

I would that I had, as your Honor has, fkill—
I know you're *Ex*-Mayor but we *honor* you ftill.
To prefent in its moft meritorious mood
Our truthful regard for the Fair and the Good.

That Collation, "got up" in fuch exquifite fenfe,
With no kind of regard to time, trouble, expenfe,
Was eaten by us, with commendable Grace,
And the funlight of Pleafure illumined each Face.
But the countenance mirrors or falfifies part
Of the genuine impulfe that reigns in the Heart.
For one thing was wanting. It's hard to remind
A Committee, moft truly, proverbially, kind,
That we needed fome object, not ready at hand.
Methinks that I hear them of *me*, make demand —
Pray, what would you have, Sir, were not the meats good?
Et cetera, et cetera, of queftions a flood —

73

This folicitude anxious, I hafte to relieve —
The Garden of Eden was sad without Eve.

But even as he who receives a rare Prize,
Which for Reafons judicious was hid from his eyes,
Rejoices the more when permitted to gaze
On what had withdrawn its magnificent Blaze,
So our Joy is complete in the beautiful fight
Which the Box of *our* theatre offers to-night.

  May I fpeak with more precifion
      To thefe Gentlemen in buff;
  Or is it your Decifion
      That I have faid enough?
  At my lines that were fatirical
      They fmiled in merry Mood;
  And fome Stanzas that are lyrical
      May fuit a foberer mood.

  Honor to them who bravely ftood,
    While yet their Realm was young,
  And drew the keen, defiant Blade,
    Or fpoke with fearlefs Tongue.

  Proud Hiftory calls her lengthened Roll
    Of Patriots and Peers;
  And brighter gleams the fhining Scroll,
    As fly the added years.

  Rhode Ifland tells with honeft pride
    Of him, her noble Son,
  Great in the Council, and the Field,
    The friend of Wafhington —
  Connecticut prefents her claim
    To many a facred leaf,
  And boafts the pure and brilliant Fame
    Of him her Hero-chief.

  A health unto Connecticut
    The Land that honors toil —

A welcome to her gallant Sons
Who tread Rhode Ifland's foil—
Come Brothers, braid a laurel Wreath
Here, at our feftive fcene,
To circle round the deathlefs Names
Of Putnam and of Greene.

The Toaſt-maſter announced that he had received from *Hon.* Wm. W. Hoppin, ex-Gov. of Rhode Ifland, *Hon.* John Pitman, U. S. Diſtrict Judge, John Whipple, Efq., one of the oldeft and ableft members of the Rhode Ifland bar, *Hon.* Wm. R. Staples, ex-Judge of the Supreme Court, E. N. Hazard, Efq., and many other prominent Gentlemen of Providence, refponfes of regret at their inability to accept the invitation to be prefent and join in the feftivities of the Occafion. A portion of the Letters read are appended:

From Ex-Gov. Hoppin.

Providence, Oct. 10*th*, 1859.

Gentlemen:—I returned to the City on Saturday afternoon laſt, and this morning find upon my defk your polite invitation to attend the Levee at Pratt's Hall, given in honor of the Putnam Phalanx. I regret that the non-reception of your note fhould have prevented my being prefent at the Banquet, and efpecially fo, as Mr. Stuart and other Gentlemen of the Phalanx are friends of mine, and whom to have met on fo pleafant an Occafion would have been mutually agreeable.

I congratulate you upon the Succefs of your Entertainment and all the Ceremonies of the Reception, which were alike diſtinguiſhed by fuperior Tafte and a large hearted Hofpitality.

Very truly Yours,
W. W. HOPPIN.

To Wm. W. Brown,
L. C. Warner,
E. C. Davis, } *Committee.*
H. Staples,
F. J. Sheldon,

FROM HON. JOHN PITMAN.
Providence, Oct. 6th, 1859.

GENTLEMEN:—I thank you for your polite invitation to the Levee of the Firſt Light Infantry in honor of the Putnam Phalanx, this evening. It would afford me much pleaſure to attend on this Occaſion, but I have found it neceſſary for my health for ſeveral years, to decline all invitations to Evening Parties, and regret therefore, that I muſt requeſt that you will have me excuſed.

I am very reſpectfully,
Your Obedient Servant,
JOHN PITMAN.

TO WM. W. BROWN,
L. C. WARNER,
E. C. DAVIS, } *Committee.*
H. STAPLES,
F. J. SHELDON,

FROM JOHN WHIPPLE, ESQ.
Committee of the Firſt Light Infantry, Providence, R. I.

GENTLEMEN:—I moſt truly regret that temporary ill health will prevent my being preſent at the reception of our Military friends from Connecticut. I regret this the more as Connecticut is one of my beau ideal States, and her People generally approaching a little nearer my Standard of a plain but ſtrong, intellectual and moral People than any that I find in ancient or modern Hiſtory. I ſhould feel proud in doing honor to any portion of the Repreſentatives of ſuch a People, more eſpecially to that portion ready at any moment to fall in the front Ranks, and pour out their blood to its laſt drop in Defence of New England men, New England law, and New England freedom.

I am, Gentlemen, moſt reſpectfully Yours,
JOHN WHIPPLE.
Providence, 5th October, 1859.

FROM HON. W. R. STAPLES.
Providence, Oct. 6th, 1859.

GENTLEMEN:—It would afford me great pleaſure to attend the Levee of the Firſt Light Infantry this evening, if I were burdened with fewer Years, or bleſſed with better Health. As it is, pleaſe ex-

cufe my abfence and accept my beft wifhes that the Infantry may on this and all other Occafions meet with the Succefs they richly merit.
With many thanks for your polite invitation,
I am, Gentlemen, your Corp'l,
W. R. STAPLES.
Col. W. W. Brown and others,
Commander F. L. Infantry.

From E. N. Hazard, Esq.

Providence, Oct. 6th, 1859.

Gentlemen:— Owing to my abfence, your note of 3d did not reach me till this morning. Nothing would have given me greater Pleafure than to have been prefent at your moft patriotic and joyous Feftival.

From all that I read and hear of the Occafion, it was well worthy the time-honored and juftly merited Reputation of the Firft Light Infantry. The Corps, in thus adding another bond of ftrength to the faft growing friendfhip between the two beautiful Cities of New England, have gained much high praife. The Corps, in this diftinguifhed act of State Courtefy and generous Hofpitality, deferve well, not only of Providence and Rhode Ifland, but of all New England. It has done more to cement the Ties of Brotherhood and good feeling between Connecticut and Rhode Ifland than any other one thing in the laft quarter of a Century. This fpirit of cordial, friendly Intercourfe fhould be nurtured and cherifhed. The time may come when it will be needed in action as it was in '76.

Pleafe accept for yourfelf and your affociates my moft refpectful regards.
Your Obedient Servant,
E. N. HAZARD.
To *Col.* Wm. W. Brown,
and others of the Committee.

To the fentiment "*The Clergy*," the *Rev.* Afher Moore, Chaplain to the Putnam Phalanx, refponded as follows:

Mr. Commandant:— I ftand here in a pofition which properly belongs to another. The voice of your own Chaplain fhould have been heard, in refponfe to the toaft juft given, before the utterance of a word by your prefent Speaker. But I ftill cheerfully obey the call that has been made upon me. I suppose that the Programme of the Occasion would be deemed incomplete, without the sound of the Chaplain's voice, and an exhibition of his venerable person.

You now see before you the first Chaplain of the Putnam Phalanx in full costume, with the exception of his Chapeau. If my Grandchildren (and I have one,) cannot look back with pride and trace their Ancestry to the illustrious Hero whose name we bear, they can at least glory in the fact that their Grandfather was the first Chaplain of the Putnam Phalanx.

My venerable person is sacredly guarded and protected by the valiant Man who is always at my left hand, that I should not be moved. He is not permitted to draw his sword for warlike purposes except in defence of the Chaplain. And he is therefore quick to perceive the approach of danger in this particular direction. Why, Sir, if any rude Assailant should come towards me with threatening Aspect, exposing my venerable person to the smallest danger, my redoubtable left hand Man would instantly unsheath his sword, and wield it with tremendous Valor, and some — *noise*.

Sir, it was my fortune to be born and reared under the shadow of Independence Hall. I early caught the Spirit of Freedom and a deep love for my Country. And to this day I have regarded Patriotism as one of the noblest virtues of an American Citizen. I do not belong to that class of the Clergy who stand in the High Places of the Church, and "make it their earnest work and daily toil" to abuse our Country, and to revile the Government by which we are all protected in our persons, in our liberties, and in our pursuits of happiness! With such "*Reformers*" I hold no fellowship. And I am happy whenever a fitting occasion offers to "lift up a Standard against them," and to repudiate their "*reforms.*"

Let our People, and especially our Children and Youth, be taught to appreciate our National blessings. Let the Pulpit, as in the olden time, be numbered among the sure Defences of our beloved Country. Let Religion and Patriotism be one and inseparable. Let the several members of this great Confederacy ever constitute The *United* States of America. And may God, the high and mighty Ruler of Heaven and Earth, ever bless "this land of the Free and home of the Brave."

In conclusion he offered the following sentiment:

The City of Providence — Though presided over by Knight, may it glow even in the light of the noontide Sun of Prosperity and Peace.

The Chaplain having, as will be noted, pointedly alluded to the Surgeon of the Phalanx and his valiant Sword and noify defence of his (the Chaplain's) perfon— and the Toaft-mafter, too, having called for fomething on the minor key, Dr. Miner promptly responded:

"Every word," he commenced by faying, "of this excellent Chaplain is replete with Eloquence and Erudition. At Bunker Hill his words were as cogent as thofe of Cicero. To-night he has exhibited a little of that keen Satire which Lawyers fometimes ufe, and that can only be difcovered by the twinkle of the left eye—all of which was evidently defigned to bring Surgeon Miner to his feet and the Platform. All who know me are aware that I am not a Speech-maker. The fphere of my activities has ever been devoted to other and different objects. I am the only Member of the Putnam Phalanx who has had the honor of being connected with your Univerfity—having been graduated in the Medical Department in 1824. I am quite familiar with your claffic Halls and claffic *Hills,* and all the beauties of Nature and Art that furround you. With regard to my military Hiftory, I refer you to the Bureau of Penfions, at Wafhington, where you will find my name amongft thofe who have received penfions in Bounty Lands for volunteer fervices to our Country in the War of 1812.

I have had the fpecial charge of the Putnam Phalanx for the paft fix months as the "Medicine-man of the Tribe." In our good old-fafhioned plain way of living, I have had no difficulty in preferving their Health—as you fee; and the Corps have always, to a man, been ready for Duty, until we arrived in Bofton. There, owing to that extravagant and bountiful courfe of living, to which the plain Yeomanry of Connecticut were unaccuftomed, three of our Corps were proftrated. Three times, therefore, was the Surgeon called from his retirement to prefcribe *fecundem artem* for the fick lift. Believing, as I always have, that the beft Mode for quelling any Infurrection or Invafion, whether by difeafe or otherwife, is, firft to fire Bullets and afterwards Blank-cartridges, I always adopt this courfe; and if I do not diflodge the Enemy on the fecond charge I am no longer the Surgeon of the Putnam Phalanx.

We have been told in Bofton, "how fweet it is to die for one's

Country." In this matter I have had no experience; but I know how glorious it is to *live* for one's Country, efpecially when we live as we are living now.

I am happy now to prefent to you every Member of this Organization in good Health and fit for Duty—ready to do Battle at any and all times whenever our Country fhall require our fervices; and I affure you that at the end of the Battle, every Man of the Phalanx will be found at his Poft, either among the Dead or the Living.

Dr. McKnight, of Providence, alfo refponded for the Doctors, in the following words:

REMARKS OF DR. MCKNIGHT.

Col. Brown, and Gentlemen of the Putnam Phalanx:—There will be no doubt in any of your minds, after I have done fpeaking, that I tell you the truth when I fay I am entirely unprepared to make a fpeech on an Occafion like this. The fact is, I feel now as did the Irifhman under fimilar circumftances, and like him, I would be willing to hold anybody's hat who would fpeak for me. Another reafon may be given for a poor Speech at this time of night, and that is, that all the beft Thunder has been ufed up. Why *Colonel,* I can juft call the names right out of Gentlemen prefent who faid juft exactly what I might, could or would have faid, had I been fortunate enough to have preceded them.

And why it is that we poor Doctors are always, on Occafions like this, called upon laft, is more than I can tell. One confolation we have at any rate, that there *has been* a time in all your lives, when the Doctor was the firft man to be called for, and when, for the time being, he became "Sir Oracle."

Although the beft Thunder has been effectually ufed up, it is not too late for me to offer in the name of the Firft Light Infantry, the right Hand of Fellowfhip to our Friends from Connecticut, and bid you a Soldier's hearty welcome to our feftive board.

Our Southern Friends have often fneeringly alluded to yours, as the Nutmeg State; if fo, then all the States fouth of Mafon's and Dixon's line, combined, would not be cute enough to make a grater.

This is not the place, nor am I the man, to review her Hiftory;— abler hands than mine have given us, in pictures of living light, memories of her Statefmen, Warriors, Orators and Poets, which time will only ferve to make brighter; let me, in paffing, fpeak of another clafs whofe memories alfo fhall endure while Time fhall be meafured by the Dial-plate and pendulum. I mean her world-renowned Mechanics.

Among them all, none have a more world-wide fame than a member of your own Company, and it may not be improper in this place, to name one who has fettled more difputes, in Love and War, by the weight of his arguments, than any other living man; for who, with a profpect of a bullet in from Colt, would wait for his kicks, before—like Captain Scott's coon, he came down. And if "Brevity is the foul of wit," then too, he is a witty man; for his reports, though fometimes repeated, are never long, and his prefcriptions fimple and efficacious as our friend Surgeon Miner's, only a fmall powder and a little pill, and like the Surgeon's, fure to kill twice out of three times.

I don't think I ever regretted being born where I was, until our late vifit to Norwich, and then I came to the conclufion that a man might juft as well not have been born at all, as to have been born outfide of Connecticut. And why? In the firft place there was Governor B., (probably a defcendant of the gentleman who was made a head fhorter by Richard 3d,) who was born there, and was very glad of it; then our good Governor Turner, (may his fhadow never be lefs) had an Aunt born there, (the Governor fays to-night twins, and I cheerfully make this correction for the benefit of pofterity, in cafe they fhould ever want to *re*-Turner,) and he was glad of it; and finally our worthy Mayor went all the way from Rhode Ifland to Connecticut on purpofe to be born there, and as that was the firft great thing he had done he was more pleafed than both Governors put together, though I don't fee that it amounted to much, for it was Knight after all, and couldn't have made much difference. So after hearing all thefe things, and feeing how much people made by being born in Connecticut, and how big fome of them grow, (*vide* the Enfign of the Phalanx,) and how tall fome of them are, (*vide* the Major of ditto,) and what an everlafting clever fet of Fellows they all are, and how pleafed they all are that they were born in Connecticut, I made up my mind that if I ever was born again, it fhould be in Connecticut, and fomewhere in the neighborhood of Norwich or Hartford.

And now, Gentlemen, as there are lots of thunder left to be difcharged, I beg leave to clofe with the following fentiment:

Col. Colt—The Author of a new and convincing ftyle of Epistol-ary Correfpondence.

Geo. H. Clark, Efq., of Hartford, (who was with the Phalanx at Bofton, but was obliged to return home without accompanying them to Providence,) fent the following poetical Toaft for this Occafion:

> Fill up to the Name of our own noble Hero —
> The man who delighted in Danger to revel;
> Who hated old Gage as the Romans did Nero,
> And feared neither Tyrant, nor fhe-wolf, nor devil,
> To Him who leapt chafms that paled old Campaigners;
> Whofe Sword, like the Lightning, flafhed Death and Difmay;
> Whofe Skill and Example turned holiday Trainers
> To the refolute Soldiers of Bunker Hill's day.
> Fill, fill to the Name of the Soldier fublime,
> Whofe Fame only brightens and broadens by Time!

To the fentiment "*The Rhode Ifland Bar*," Benj. F. Thurfton, Efq., of Providence, made an able refponfe, and clofed with the following toaft:

> *The Bonds of the Cities of Providence and Hartford*—The *Principal*, the interchange of kindly courtefies; the principal to be paid only at the expiration of Eternity: the guaranty of that interchange of kindly and generous fentiment, by that beft Guerdon of Good Faith, fair and open rivalry.

A Gueft offered this fentiment:

> *The Senate of the State of Rhode Ifland.*

Hon. Samuel Currey, a State Senator of Rhode Ifland, was called upon by the Toaft-mafter, and refponded as follows:

REMARKS OF HON. SAMUEL CURREY.

Mr. Col. Commander:—I am forry, amidft the general joy of this Occafion, to raife any voice of complaint, but I feel that I muft enter my proteft againft the Conqueft that has been made of me this evening. When a few hours fince, thefe buff-booted Strangers entered here unarmed and took their feats befide us, I could not have imagined I was fo foon to be made their Captive. I had before known fomething of the force of Eloquence, but I had not known what danger there may be in the voice of a *Judge Advocate* and an *Affiftant Commiffary*. Truly there muft be fome wizard enchantment thrown over us, fome magic fpell, perhaps, floating in the atmofphere that we breathe in this Hall. I own myfelf quite overcome by the fafcinations of the brilliant Oratory, the graceful Compliments to our State and her Inftitutions, and the yet more graceful Sentiments with which we have been entertained by your Guefts. Still, Sir, if I can, for a little time, difpel the charm of thefe magic arts, it will give me the greateft pleafure, both on my own account and in behalf of our State Senate for which I am to fpeak, to unite my voice with the general Welcome which we give to the Putnam Phalanx. We are all pleafed to make their acquaintance in this their martial attire, and to admire in them that Public Spirit and patience of difcipline which have drawn together and formed fo fine a body of Citizen Soldiers.

I have often, Sir, fince our two Cities of Hartford and Providence have been brought near to each other by the iron horfe, looked forward to many reunions of their people, but I had not anticipated the gratification of a vifit from a Military Company embodying fo much of the intelligence, character and focial worth of our neighboring City. I may certainly in all fobriety fay that this Martial Body of men, compofed of the venerable in character and years — the Fathers of their City — the proper Reprefentatives of all the Arts, Bufinefs and Walks of life — is a beautiful object of admiration as well as a moft inftructive fubject of reflection. I am fure that all our People take pleafure in doing honor to fuch Guefts. I am fure that the Chief Magiftrates of our City and State, whom we fee here this evening, truly reprefent the feelings of all the Citizens in the cordial greetings which they have given to our Friends from Hartford; and if our Legiflature had happened to be in feffion here at this time, you would have feen the Reprefentatives of the whole People paying refpect to that confervative love of Order which has formed, and the Patriotic Spirit which animates the Putnam Phalanx.

The People of Rhode Ifland and their Government have had experience of the neceffity, at times, of an arm of power to give ftrength to the voice of the Law. I remember going once as a meffenger, in a crifis of our domeftic Hiftory, to our late *Governor* King, to inform him of an organized refiftance to the Civil Authorities. We had not at that time the admirable organization of Military Companies which is now fo much the object of our juft pride as well as ground of reliable fecurity; and I fhall never forget how that man of iron nerve and will, in view of the imminency and magnitude of the danger and the powerleffnefs of the Civil Magiftrate, wrung his hands as he exclaimed—"I *wifh we had a little more force.*" Now it is for the purpofe of providing for the State againft the time in which her dark hour of danger may come, this "little more force," that thefe thoughtful men of Connecticut have organized themfelves under the Law as Citizen Soldiers. Their martial Array and Difcipline are not alone for Summer-day fhow and Parade. Thefe pleafing difplays have a fober meaning and ufeful fignificance. They teach us that when the hour of peril comes thefe men will be prepared to go forth and meet it, whether it be from a Domeftic or Foreign Enemy, and that they will meet the Enemy, not as mercenary Soldiers, but as brave men having an intereft of their own in the conflict.

But I am admonifhed, Mr. Commander, by this midnight hour not to try your patience with a Speech, and there is the lefs occafion for my doing it after fo many eloquent addreffes from the gentlemen who have preceded me. I will therefore only further fay that we fhall all long remember this Occafion, and long affociate in our minds many pleafing recollections of an evening with the Putnam Phalanx.

Let me offer the following fentiment:

The Putnam Phalanx—Old Fogies, rivalling in the precifion and activity of their martial exercifes the elafticity and vigor of Young America.

The following volunteer fentiment—

Woman—The true Infpirer of true Patriotifm—

Was refponded to by H. L. Miller, formerly *Major* of the 1ft Company Governor's Foot Guard of Connecticut, as follows:

REMARKS BY COL. H. L. MILLER.

Mr. Chairman:—Sergeant Sill has been fummoned to refpond to the Toaft juft read. In his abfence my name has been called. It is faid that Sergeant Sill is with the Ladies. Happy man—I wifh I was with them myfelf. Or rather, I wifh they were with me. Or, better ftill, I wifh they were with *us*, here at thefe tables, inftead of being feparated and fhut up in yonder Gallery.

It has truly gladdened our Hearts to enjoy their prefence. We have been charmed with the beautiful fight; but, oh, how delightful, if your arrangements had permitted their mingling with us, at this Feftive Board.

I cannot attempt a refponfe to the fentiment juft offered, at this late hour. Indeed it is prefumption in me, after the foul-ftirring ftrains of Eloquence poured forth in fuch rich profufion here to-night, to even permit the found of my voice to be heard.

The Putnam Phalanx, it is faid, is a peculiar Organization, and this Excurfion is for peculiar enjoyment. We *are* organized as a peculiar Battalion of Infantry, of Heavy Infantry, if you pleafe fo to defignate us, and I may fay, without vanity, that we bring with us fome heavy Ordnance. This peculiarity I know you will admit. You have heard the roar of our Artillery. You have heard the booming of our big Guns. And now, forfooth, you would hear from the Mufketry. Well, I may fay for myfelf, and for others, that we muft all anfwer to our names when called. We never turn our backs on Friend or Foe. The Auftrian Soldiers, after a recent Battle, when carried to the Hofpitals, were turned upon their faces, to have their wounds dreffed. We can take no fuch pofition. We never allow a fire in the rear. Our kind hearted, fympathizing Surgeon, has given timely notice, that he will drefs no fuch inglorious wounds. The "glorious Scar upon the Brow," would be his only Trophy, as well as our own. We cannot run. We muft ftand in our lot. We muft do or die.

Mr. Chairman, you are overwhelming us with Kindnefs. Your Hofpitality is unbounded. We know this is prompted by your true and friendly impulfes, but perhaps you have had an eye to your own fafety, and that of your City, in this frank and generous Reception. We certainly came here, to renew, and to ftrengthen, and to cultivate Friendfhips, and to draw clofer the Bond of Brotherhood between our refpective Cities.

But we came here confcious of our ftrength. We can take Cities, fubdue Kingdoms, and perform prodigies of valor generally. It was propofed, while we were on Bunker Hill, that we fhould take back with us to Hartford, every granite Block of which that Monument is compofed, and again erect it on Wyllys's Hill, in place of the noble old Charter Oak that has recently paffed away. We could have done it; not a Man of us doubted our ability. You, Sir, and others, who now fit around thefe Tables, as you look upon the empty diſhes, will admit that ſince we came into this Hall, we have appropriated to ourſelves a Bunker Hill monument of food. You thus have ſome evidence of our Capacity, but you can hardly imagine what evils might have befallen your beautiful and proſperous City, if we had come down upon you in hoſtile array.

You have, however, diſarmed us. You have given us a view of your inner Life, and we are enchanted. You have made us your Friends forever. We embrace you as Brethren. We ſhall always retain a pleaſant Remembrance of your Courteſy and Kindneſs. We ſhall treaſure in our Hearts the recollection of this viſit to Providence, and, on our return Home, ſhall wait with impatience for an opportunity to give evidence of our Gratitude, when, as Soldiers, or Citizens, you may hereafter viſit our City of Hartford.

A ſentiment complimentary to the Artillery of the Marines and the Marine Artillery, which thundered a welcome to the Putnam Phalanx, called up *Lt. Col.* Tompkins, who made a brief and moſt happy reſponſe, concluding with the ſentiment—

The True Soldier—Like Iſrael Putnam—ever ready to do—to dare—to die.

The following ſentiment, offered by *Commiſſary* Rodman, was drank in ſilence, ſtanding:

The Memory of Barber and Childs—The Infantry mourns the loſs of theſe moſt popular and efficient Members.

Capt. A. M. Gordon, of the Second Company of the Putnam Phalanx, in alluſion to the uniform of the Firſt Light Infantry, offered the following:

The Firſt Light Infantry—We know they are Soldiers—they ought to be Scholars—for they are deeply red and ſlightly blue.

Shortly after twelve o'clock, the aſſembled Company roſe from the tables, and the Phalanx were eſcorted to their Quarters at the Earl Houſe, by their Hoſts of the evening.

The Members of the Phalanx take this opportunity to place on permanent Record their unqualified approbation and cordial appreciation of the admirable and effective manner in which all the arrangements for this feſtive Occaſion were conceived and carried out. Nothing ſeemed wanting. The Entertainment itſelf was more than elegant. Our Hoſts, the Firſt Light Infantry, may well claim to be "an Hoſt in themſelves." Our warmeſt thanks are due to that Galaxy of Ladies who graced the ſcene with their fair preſence; to the diſtinguiſhed Gueſts who reſponded to the invitation and were preſent to add their words of Welcome and Congratulation; to the American Braſs Band, whoſe moſt excellent Muſic added ſo much to the enjoyment of the evening; and to all, whoſe efforts were devoted to rendering this the fineſt Feſtival of the ſort that ever occurred in Providence. The memories of this Evening are among the choiceſt connected with the entire Excurſion.

At half-paſt eight o'clock on Friday morning the Phalanx, eſcorted by the Infantry, left their Quarters and marched to Brown Univerſity, which they had been invited to viſit by the Authorities of that Inſtitution. Upon entering Rhode Iſland Hall, they were received by the Preſident and Faculty of the Univerſity. Preſident Sears, in a moſt felicitous manner, gave them a cordial Welcome to the Academic Halls. He aſſured them that they were not ſtrangers here. "Many of your number," ſaid he, "are known to us as public Men, who have been juſtly honored by being called to important official ſtations in your own city and State. And we, as

a Literary Inftitution, have not been flow to obferve that
you have eloquent Orators and elegant Scholars among
the Officers and Members of your Company, exemplify-
ing moft appropriately and beautifully the value of that
Culture which we aim to reach in our humble labors
here. We welcome you as the friends of Learning and
the ornaments of Society, who have contributed much
to the high reputation of your honored City." Judging
from the uniform which the Phalanx fo gracefully wore,
he thought it would not be unpleafant to them to learn
that the Soldiers of the Revolution ufed their oldeft College Edifice for a barrack and hofpital. In the name of
the Old College, therefore, he would greet them as
Brethren of the Revolution of '76.

To this cordial Welcome of Prefident Sears, *Judge
Advocate* Stuart refponded as follows:

Prefident Sears:—For the truly cordial and complimentary remarks with which you welcome the Putnam Phalanx to thefe Academic
Shades and to this beautiful and fuggeftive Hall, its Members defire,
through me, to return you their warmeft thanks.

It is true, Sir, as you remark, that we come here clad in the pano-
ply of the Revolutionary Days. Our Battalion has been formed from
the ftirring incentive of thofe Days, and for a high and patriotic End.
We defire through our peculiar Drefs, and Difcipline, and Mufical
Corps, to revive and ftrengthen thofe thoughts and affociations which
clufter around the great Paft of our Liberty. We would fain ftimulate the Love of Country. By a contemplation of the toil, and treasure, and blood, which founded our maffive Republican Inftitutions,
we would aid in endearing them to the Affection and Reverence of all,
and in awakening in all the ambition to emulate the noble Virtues of
thofe venerable Patriots, thofe great and good Men, whofe Souls conceived, and whofe ftalwart hands worked out the giant problem of
American Independence.

For the purpofe of kindling anew in our own bofoms the fires of
Patriotifm, we have ourfelves juft been on a pilgrimage to Bofton and

Bunker Hill—to the Shrines of thofe illuſtrious Men, and gallant Soldiers, who there led the van of the American Revolution. And worthy Prefident, a military Battalion though we are, there is nothing incongruous in our ſtanding here in thefe Halls of Literature and Science. For, in a Republic like our own, founded on intelligence, the connection between the profeffion of Arms and Knowledge is, or always ought to be, intimate and profound. It was an educated Soldiery, Sir, that fought and won our great battles for Independence. The Men who achieved our Victories upon thefe fields were men who *knew*, knew thoroughly their Rights, and who knowing, dared maintain them. They had enjoyed a long experience of Civilization. They underſtood its bleffings—and in the light of the liberty for which they contended, and which their Valor won, determined to lay broader and deeper than ever before—in Inſtitutions efpecially of Education—in Literature, in Science, in Art, in Good Morals and Religion—the true foundation-ſtones of American Profperity and Glory.

And among our American Inſtitutions of learning, Mr. Prefident, this venerable one over which you fo ably prefide, has long, our Phalanx is happy to remark, held a confpicuous place—and, Sir, as regards education generally, the State of Rhode Ifland ſtands defervedly high. From the epoch of your firſt Schoolmaſter here in Providence —the venerable John Turpin—down to the days of your munificent educational Benefactors, the Almys and the Browns, and the eſtabliſhment of this your Univerfity, and of your admirable fyſtem of Public Schools—on, down to the prefent moment—Education has been with you a pride and a fuccefs.

Your People were among the very earlieſt in the Country to erect, at your Olneyville, a large and complete Paper-mill. Far back as 1762, you eſtabliſhed one of the very firſt Newfpapers in the Country — *The Providence Gazette*—that ſtout organ of Whig principles, and patriotic refolves, during the ever-memorable era of the Stamp Act, and the ſtill more memorable era of the American Revolution. Your Newspapers and Periodicals, many in number, and many of high merit—and grave works in moral and political Science, like thofe of your profound and venerated Wayland, and in Hiſtory, like that admirable one of your State by Arnold—have marked the intellectual appetite of your People ever fince. All America has ſtudied the Weather, and learned Meteorology, from the earlieſt among its Almanac-makers, your own venerable Isaac Bickerstaff. All America, yes, and Europe too, pays homage to the illustrious Painter of Washington, your renowned Gilbert Stuart—fitting compeer that he was, in his beautiful art, for our own immortal Painter of Connecticut—Colonel John Trumbull. And the World will ever know by heart, among the loftiest Heroes of American History, that Officer of the Revolution from your State, accomplished in mind as well as in arms—who wielded the Pen almost as skillfully as he did the Sword—Brigadier General Greene.

Sir, your University has sent forth numberless Sons, who, both at home and abroad, in various portions of our common Country, adorning their educational birth, have rendered conspicuous services in the defence of their Country, and in the cultivation of Literature and Science, and Art. The Putnam Phalanx, let me assure you, rejoices in this fact—and trusts that these Classic Halls will ever continue to furnish, for the pride of your own immediate Community, and for the just boast of your State, thousands more of educated Sons, ready and anxious to do you honor, and to bear away from among the many noble teachings of their *Alma Mater*, as the Inspiration through life of their Patriotism, the proud, undying precept of the old Roman—"*Dulce et decorum est pro Patria mori!*"

In reply, *Dr*. Sears said that the College could offer but little for their entertainment. Her chief ornament—the many Sons who had gone out from her walls and done her credit in the World—she could not now exhibit. He therefore begged the Commandant to accept a triennial Catalogue and a brief History of the College, and invited the Phalanx to visit the Library and the Grounds.

The Battalion then repaired to the Library where they were courteously received by Reuben A. Guild, the accomplished Librarian of the Institution. A brief period passed here, when the reveille announced the departure of the Corps to the fine lawn east of the College, where a promenade and interchange of courtesies ensued. The College Grounds were crowded with Spectators, and the

Bands meanwhile furnifhed moft excellent mufic. The Day itfelf was moft delightful, delicioufly cool, and bright under the October fun.

The line was formed at half paft ten o'clock, and proceeded to the refidence of *Mayor* Knight, on High ftreet. The Manfion was thronged with vifitors, among whom were many members of the City Council and of the State Government, the *Hon.* James F. Simmons, *Hon.* C. C. Van Zandt, *Captain* J. J. Comstock, many of the general Officers of the Militia of the State, the Officers of the Staff of the Marine Artillery, the Officers of the Staff of the Mechanic Rifles, and the Officers of the Staff of the Pawtucket Light Guard, and many other Gentlemen of Military and Civic diftinction. A bounteous and elegant collation was fpread in the rear of the Mayor's houfe, and as foon as the invited Guefts had found ftanding room, his Honor addreffed *Major* Goodwin of the Phalanx in a welcome fpeech, affuring him and his Command of the pleasure and gratification which their vifit to Providence had afforded its Citizens, and closing by tendering to the Phalanx the hospitalities due to the occafion and its affociations.

At the requeft of the Major Commandant, *Affiftant Commiffary* Deming refponded to this brief Welcome:

Mr. Mayor and Gentlemen:—We are met at every ftep, in this good City of Providence, with fuch profufe manifeftations of good will and Hofpitality, that words are hourly growing more and more impotent, to exprefs the fentiments of Gratitude and Obligation with which we are overwhelmed. From the moment of our Arrival, to this, the hour of our Departure, it has been a continuous Ovation, and the increafing fchedule of our debtors is becoming burdenfome, not only to our fenfibilities—grateful and refponfive,—but even to the memory. And I have been inftructed by our Major Commandant, to improve this opportunity, while the pleafing Spell is frefh upon us, to offer up the largeft Thank-offering of the Putnam Phalanx to the military Companies, public Bodies and Individuals who have participated in this Reception; to the Marine Artillery for the falvo which firft welcomed us to your borders; to our efpecial Hofts the Light Infantry and Old Guard for their unremitting contribution to our honor and enjoyment, and, particularly, for the magnificent Banquet which fittingly crowned the elegant courtefies of yefterday; to your diftinguifhed Men and daily Journals for their ample commendation of our Corps, our City, and our Commonwealth; to Prefident Sears for his invitation to your ancient Seat of Learning, and for the appropriate and cordial Speech which relieved, at once, the diffidence of Soldiers in that chofen Abode of Scholars; to your Citizens generally for their unftinted approbation of our Organization, evinced in private acts and expreffions of kindnefs, as well as in the loud and continuous plaudits, which have attended our March; to yourfelf, Mr. Mayor, for adding to the eclat of the Excurfion by your own appearance, as Soldier, in the ranks of our noble Efcort, and for throwing open your doors for our entertainment as Chief Executive of this beautiful City. Moreover, as true and faithful Knights, we vow admiration and loyalty to the charming Ladies of Providence who have loaded us with garlands and bewitched us with their graceful and enthufiaftic Welcome.

We long to evince our thankfulnefs by fomething more fignificant than words; we covet the Opportunity of reciprocating thefe lavifh Civilities, and if thofe to whom we are indebted fhall ever vifit Hartford, we will grant them the freedom of our Homes and Hearts and decorate them with every infignia of honor in the power of this Battalion to confer.

Various fentiments and brief fpeeches followed, and an hour or more was paffed moft agreeably at the tables. The adjoining refidence of *Affiftant Commiffary* Davis was also open, and the Guefts of the Mayor availed themselves of this opportunity to pay their refpects to Mr. Davis, and were received with elegant Hofpitality.

It was expected that the Phalanx would leave Providence at half-paſt two o'clock, but intelligence having been received of the intended public Reception of the Battalion on their arrival Home, it was arranged that a ſpecial Train ſhould leave Providence at one o'clock in order to arrive before dark at Hartford. This fact having been announced, the viſit to *Mayor* Knight was neceſſarily ſhortened, and at a little paſt twelve, both Companies formed in front of his reſidence and the line of march was taken up for the Depot, his Honor being saluted as the ſignal of departure with ſix hearty cheers from the Phalanx.

At the Depot an immenſe number of People had aſſembled, and while waiting a short time for the Train, a profuſion of ſplendid boquets was fairly ſhowered upon the Battalion. They were the gift of Ladies who came in perſon, with *ex-Mayor* Rodman and many friends, to preſent them to the Phalanx. The Train moved on amid loud huzzas, and the Corps left the City fully impreſſed with the now familiar fact, that Providence is one of the moſt hoſpitable Cities in New England.

The following are ſelected from the many flattering notices which were publiſhed, during the brief viſit of the Phalanx at Providence:

[From the Providence Journal.]

The Putnam Phalanx have made the moſt favorable impreſſion upon our People. Their peculiar Uniform, carrying us back to the days of the Revolution and aſſociating them with the moſt patriotic Era of our Hiſtory, their ſtirring Muſic of drums and fifes, their ſtalwart forms and manly bearing, the venerable locks of their Commander, the portly figure of their Standard bearer, all called forth continual admiration as they marched through the ſtreets lined with Spectators. We do not remember any Military Diſplay that has given more ſatisfaction in our City.

[From the Prov. Cor. of the Bofton Journal.]

No body of Military ever received at the hands of the Militia of Rhode Ifland fuch fumptuous entertainment, and fuch profufe outpouring of Welcome, as has been accorded to the Putnam Phalanx of Hartford during the fhort vifit of the Corps to this City. Everything that a liberal hand could adminifter has been beftowed upon the gallant Company with the charaɛteriftic generofity of Rhode Ifland Soldiers. The bounteous Hofpitality of Bofton has been repeated here, and every feature of the Occafion has been carried forward with eminent Succefs.

On arriving at the Moofup Station, an incident occurred which in its touching fimplicity was the moft affeɛting of all that happened during the entire Excurfion. Mary Putnam Holbrook, daughter of J. Holbrook, Efq., of Brooklyn, and great-great-grand-daughter of *Gen.* Ifrael Putnam—an exceedingly pretty and interefting child of fourteen years, was in waiting with a beautiful Wreath with which fhe defired to crown the Commander of the Phalanx bearing the name of her honored Anceftor. Upon learning the circumftance, the Major Commandant with his Staff and many of the Rank and File affembled upon the platform of the Depot, when the young Lady placed the Wreath upon the neck of the Major Commandant and faluted him with a cordial kifs. The accompanying Note, at the requeft of the Major Commandant was read by *Judge Advocate* Stuart to the Phalanx:

"Pleafe accept this wreath from a Defcendant of Gen. PUTNAM. Some of the flowers are frefh from his grave in Brooklyn, eight miles diftant.

"MARY PUTNAM HOLBROOK, of Brooklyn, Ct."

Mr. STUART then faid:—I am commiffioned by the Major Commandant of the Putnam Phalanx to return you, my dear Child, his heart-felt Thanks for this manifeftation of your intereft in the Battalion which he commands. Some of your Flowers, fays the note, "are frefh from the Grave" of Gen. Putnam. Thought touching indeed to the Hearts of us all! This Phalanx has been, Mary, upon a long and delightful Excurfion. It has received many and bountiful expreffions of the public Regard. Wreaths after Wreaths have been fhowered upon the brows of its Officers and Soldiers; but no one of them, let me affure you, has been received with emotions fo deep as this one with which you have now crowned our veteran Commander.

It comes with peculiar propriety from you, Child—for in your veins flows the blood of that Hero whofe great name this Phalanx bears, and whofe memory, as one of the moft patriotic and gallant Leaders of the American Revolution, it is our purpofe to ftrengthen and perpetuate. He was a Man who ventured everything for his Country. He gave to it, without ftint, his blood and his treafure, and we defire that all fhould love and honor your illuftrious Anceftor, fweet Child, as you do.

Again, for our Major Commandant, and for all the Officers and Soldiers of his command, I thank you for this warm-hearted Teftimonial of your regard for our happinefs and fuccefs in the efforts we make to ftimulate the noble Love of Country, and to awaken admiration for the heroic Men who achieved that Revolution which made our Land, in the grandeft fenfe of the familiar, but ever endeared and endearing words, emphatically "the Land of the Free and the Home of the Brave." *You* certainly fhow that you feel the force of thofe fublime Strains which conftitute the Infpiration of the impofing Battalion now before you:

> "Our native Country, thee—
> Land of the noble Free—
>   Thy Name we love.
> We love thy rocks and rills,
> Thy woods and templed hills;
> Land where our Fathers died—
> Land of the Pilgrim's pride—
> From every mountain fide
>   Let Freedom ring!"

And now, in the name and behalf of the Putnam Phalanx, fweet Benefactrefs, for the falutation which you fo handfomely beftowed on our veteran Commander, I return you a parting, cordial kifs. Good bye—God blefs you!

In refponfe to this eloquent Addrefs, Mr. Holbrook, father of Mifs Mary, faid:

It is hardly neceffary, *Major* Goodwin, for me, the Father of this little Girl, to apologize for her inability to refpond in an appropriate Manner to the feeling and truly beautiful remarks of the Hon. Judge Advocate in behalf of the Battalion. The detention of the Train and the alighting of the Phalanx has taken us entirely by furprife, and we all feel highly honored. As the Train is already "behind time," I will only fay that I deeply regret that the Phalanx has no "Daughter of the Regiment" that I might reciprocate the hearty kifs beftowed by your noble and eloquent Judge Advocate. It is hardly poffible, however, Sir, knowing what I do of the refined taftes of the individual Members of the Phalanx, to induce me to believe that under any ordinary circumftances, they would be fatisfied with this novel procefs of kiffing by proxy. I thank you for your kind Acceptance of my daughter's Tribute to your Battalion, and in her behalf, my own, and of many prefent, exprefs the warmeft wifhes for the Succefs and Profperity of the Putnam Phalanx.

The whole affair was fo unexpected, and yet, of fuch a moving, tender character, that the feelings of the entire Phalanx and affembled Throng were touched, and the Train moved on midft mingled cheers and tears. The following touching Lines upon the Event are from the pen of George H. Clark, Efq.:

 Flowers from his Grave—and by his Grandchild brought!
  What Emblems more could fanctify the Scene?
 Then was each Soul with tender Memories fraught,
  Evoked by Her who bore that Garland green;
 Strong men forgot their boafted Manhood then,
  And Eyes that feldom wept, with Tears were dim,—
 In War's grim guife her Grandfire conquered men,
  She, with thefe frail Memorials of Him.

 Was not his fhadowy Prefence near her there,
  The while fhe plucked thofe Leaves and Bloffoms wild?

And did not Seraphs, hovering in the air,
Pronounce a Benediction on the Child?
They furely did—for, ftill unfeen but feeing,
The air is rife with their fuftaining Power,
And, all intenfified, her fentient Being
Commuced with His in that moft Holy Hour.

FROM GRAVE TO GAY.

The *Providence Journal*, in commenting upon this Incident remarks, in a quiet way, as thus:

"In one marked inftance, however, Mr. Stuart in fpeaking for *Major* Goodwin, went quite beyond the line of delegated Duty, and fet up for himfelf, in a manner which, if the Major is the Difciplinarian we take him for, will bring the offender to a Court-martial. It was well enough when Mifs Holbrook placed a Wreath on the Commander's head, and a kifs on his lips, that Mr. Stuart fhould reply "on behalf of Major Goodwin;" it was well enough when, "on behalf of *Major* Goodwin," he thanked the Grand-daughter of *General* Putnam for her floral Gift; it was well enough when, "on behalf of *Major* Goodwin," he told her what a Good Time they had had in Bofton and Providence; but when, ftill further, "on behalf of *Major* Goodwin," he returned the Kifs on the Lady's own lips, it feems to us that the indignant Major might well have exclaimed, that however his Judge Advocate might excel him in making Speeches, there were fome little things appertaining to his Command that he could attend to himfelf. We expect to fee in the Hartford papers an order for a Court-martial; and although a great deal is doubtlefs to be faid in the way of extenuation, the offence is one that no Commander who has a proper idea of his Duties and his Rights can be expected to overlook."

At various points on the route homewards the Phalanx was faluted. At Baltic, the Operatives in the immenfe Mill waved their welcomes from every window, and the arrival of the Train at each Station was the fignal for a gathering, and everywhere the Corps was greeted with enthufiafm.

Between Andover and Bolton the Engine gave out and the Train was delayed three hours or more — the *only* annoying circumftance of the entire Excurfion. The regular evening Train from Providence came along and brought the Phalanx to Hartford.

THE RECEPTION AT HOME.

The Citizens of Hartford, not unmindful of the Honor conferred upon the City by the diftinguifhed regard with which their "Representative Men" had been received at Bofton, Charleftown and Providence, refolved to publicly receive the Phalanx home again in an appropriate and becoming manner. The Affair was almoft *impromptu*. Yet, at the time of the expected arrival, at 5.20 p. m., on Friday, Oct. 7th, the Light Guard, under the command of *Capt.* Levi Woodhoufe, the Seymour Light Artillery, *Capt.* Horace Ensworth, Commandant, with the Hartford Cornet Band, the Members of the Common Council, and an immenfe concourfe of Citizens were in waiting at the Station to welcome home once more the Phalanx. The prolonged and unaccountable delay of the Train produced much anxiety left fome accident of ferious character might have happened, but at laft, at eight o'clock, a gun from the Park announced the arrival. The Battalion was received by their Military Efcort and marched up Afylum through Trumbull, Church and Main ftreets to the State Houfe, where a hollow fquare was formed — the Phalanx in the centre.

It was eminently fitting that our diftinguifhed Fellow-citizen, *Ex-Gov.* Thos. H. Seymour, who but a few weeks before had himfelf received a Public Reception, after fix years of abſence, from his Fellow Citizens—in which Ovation the Phalanx took a prominent part—ſhould now in turn be called upon to welcome home the Phalanx. He was accordingly introduced to the Battalion by *Capt.* Enſworth, and in behalf of the Eſcort and his Fellow-citizens addreſſed them.

Gov. Seymour's Welcome.

Major Goodwin, and Members of the Putnam Phalanx:—A few weeks ſince, on my return to this City, I received a moſt friendly Welcome from a Member of your Corps, in language ſo eloquent that it forbade a ſuitable reply on my part.

To-night the circumſtances are changed. It is *you* who have come to *us*—for I am again one of the number of your Fellow-citizens— and upon me has fallen the diſtinguiſhed Honor of receiving you in the heart of our honored City. I welcome you Home in the name and in behalf of the fine Military Eſcort which has come with you to the place where you now ſtand; in behalf of the crowd of Citizens you ſee gathered around you on every ſide; in the name of hoſts of Neighbors and Friends, and of your Fellow-citizens generally—in the name and behalf of all theſe, I heartily welcome the Phalanx back to Hartford.

We meaſure Time, it is ſaid, by *Events*, rather than by Hours and Days. Tried by this ſtandard, your viſit to Bunker Hill has a deep ſignificance. It is an Event. It has come to be hiſtoric; ſomething worthy of all remembrance. You have been there, not as individuals merely, but as a Corps;—you wore the Coſtume of '76; you bore the honored name of PUTNAM on your Banner; you carried in your boſoms the glorious Memories of the Times in which he lived, and the Scenes in which he was engaged. You were not the mere Spectators of outward and viſible things, but you held Communion with the unforgotten Dead. Your viſit to the memorable Heights of Charleſtown had its fulleſt effect on you as a Corps. You have been where your Forefathers thrice repulſed the Troops of King George; when glancing your eyes down the ſlope of that Hill, you felt as they felt, when driving back the Train-bands of the King. You have ſeen, in ſpirit, the heroic Fight; you have heard the voice of the Captains, and the ſhouting. Your feet have preſſed the Ground where

Warren fell; where, from the fibrous mould, came up the words of the expiring Martyr:—"It is fweet and pleafant to die for one's Country."

Circumftances like thefe give to your vifit to Bunker Hill the character of an Event, rather than the journey of a Day. We are glad to fee you back again. Your Fellow-citizens rejoice to greet the Phalanx on this occafion of their return to the City. They are delighted with the accounts they have received of the never-to-be forgotten vifit of the Affociation to the Shrine of our Country's Independence.

It has pleafed your Fellow-citizens to hear of the attentions the Affociation has everywhere received on their way to and from Bofton —of the Welcome extended to the Phalanx by their Honors the Mayors of Bofton, and Charleftown, and Providence;—of their meeting with Mr. Everett; of the entertainment given them at Bofton by one of their valued Members;—of their Excurfion to Providence, and the very cordial Reception they were honored with at that City.

[Gov. S. reiterated the pleafure it gave their Fellow-citizens to fee the Corps fafely back again. Anxiety had been felt at the failure of the cars to arrive at the hour the Phalanx were expected—an anxiety happily removed at laft.]

Major Goodwin, your Fellow-citizens have taken the deepeft intereft in the journey of your Corps. They have followed your courfe, and rejoiced at the attentions paid you. I once more welcome you and the Members of the Phalanx to Hartford, a City which is proud of the Corps. Welcome to the fcene of your labors and of your triumphs. Long may the Phalanx maintain its prefent Strength and Organization, honored from year to year with renewed tokens of the Refpect and Confidence of their Fellow-citizens.

Major Goodwin called upon *Acting Sergeant* Sill to refpond to this Welcome:

Sergeant Sill's Reply.

Sir:—Permit me to tender you the thanks of the Putnam Phalanx for this Welcome home. We return, not with the trophies of War, like the ancient Armies who came home from Conquefts with elephants in their train bearing the fpoils of conquered Territory and pillaged Cities, but with grateful Hearts and the Victory of Peace. It is faid that the Grecians were ten years conquering Troy; but we have conquered three Cities in lefs than four days! We have entered their walls, we have fat down and eaten, we have lain down and flept within their Palaces. And we fay it with pride, though not boaftingly, that three Cities have laid down their arms before the victorious Phalanx, and the Charleftown Navy Yard opened wide its gates, though never before invaded by a Military Company.

Yet we return with a fenfe of pleafure at arriving Home, which our victories elfewhere have not excited, and with a feeling that there is indeed no fweeter place on earth than Home! Therefore it is, that we fhould be pardoned if we are more grateful for this cordial Greeting by our Friends, than for the attentions paid us elfewhere, and above all we are thankful for this fine Efcort, fo finely and kindly tendered, and your determination to await our arrival through long and anxious hours, commends your Goodnefs ftill more to our Gratitude. We feel grateful that we have, as Reprefentatives of the Citizens of Hartford, achieved a greater Victory by our peaceful Triumphs, than he that goeth forth to Battle. I believe I confine myfelf to the facts, when I fay that we have done more than any other agency, to command Refpect for our City from the places we have vifited, and to cement the Bonds of Friendfhip exifting between them, making them feel that ours were common wants, common interefts and common feelings. We thank you again for your Efcort on this occafion, and as we have enjoyed ourfelves fo well this time, and as it is natural for us to endeavor to enjoy ourfelves as much as poffible, during the brief fpace allotted us while here, it is not impoffible we may go again to Bunker Hill.

Major Commandant Goodwin advanced with the Wreath of Flowers received at Moofup Station and faid:

Fellow-citizens:—A young Lady placed thefe flowers around my neck—fome of them were plucked to-day, from the Grave of *General* Putnam!

Loud cheers were given for *Gov.* Seymour, the Efcort and the Battalion. In refponfe to an enthufiaftic call, *Judge Advocate* Stuart came forward and faid that he had almoft exhaufted his voice in refponding to the

Welcomes the Battalion had received from the people of Bofton, Charleftown and Providence, and in endeavoring to do juftice to the local and national fubjects which, at Bunker Hill and at Providence, had forced themfelves upon the notice of the Battalion. He was happy, however, to refpond to the call from his Fellow-citizens and to thank them for this endorfement of their Vifit, thereby endorfing the Principles that lie at the Bafis of all our Inftitutions and infure our Profperity. After the handfome refponfe of *Sergeant* Sill, it was unneceffary for him, he faid, to add anything to exprefs the warm appreciation of the Battalion for this fpontaneous Welcome of their Fellow-citizens. He trusted that the Phalanx in their Journeyings had been properly reprefentative of the City and had reflected Honor upon the Old Charter Oak State.

In refponfe to a call, *Affiftant Commiffary* Deming faid that it would afford him great pleafure under more favorable circumftances, to give his Fellow-citizens an account of the Reception the Battalion had met with in the Metropolis of New England, and in the hofpitable City of Providence. But, although fuch a narrative might be gratifying to thofe who had ftaid at home, it would be wearifome to the Battalion. The Phalanx have already informally refolved to put upon record, in fome permanent fhape, an Account of their memorable Expedition, and the curiofity of thofe who wifh to hear of it will be probably gratified.

Major Goodwin here called on the Battalion for three cheers for the Citizens of Hartford, which were given with a will; then, efcorted by the two Companies, the Phalanx marched to the City Hall, where, after a few words of commendation and congratulation, the Chaplain, *Rev.* Afher Moore, offered a Prayer of Thankfgiving and the Phalanx was difmiffed.

[From the Hartford Daily Times.]
RETURN OF THE PUTNAM PHALANX
FROM THEIR EXCURSION TO BOSTON AND PROVIDENCE.

Come back,—come back to us,
  Nor longer feek to roam;
We've heard your Welcome from afar,
  And give the Welcome home!
We watch'd you as you went
  With martial ftep and eye,
Your gorgeous Banner floating out
  Upon the autumnal Sky.

Your Leader at your head,
  Alert, erect and bold,
As tho' his threefcore years and ten
  Had fcarcely half been told:
Your ancient Plumes we mark'd,
  And glittering in the Sun,
The Coftume of our bleffed Sires
  Who ftood with Wafhington.

You've been at Bunker Hill,
  But not the foe to meet,
And win that blood-bought victory,
  The Britons call'd *defeat.*
Saw ye that Hero's form
  In glorious vifion there,
Whofe Name is graven on your fhield?
  Whofe Banner-ftaff ye bear?

And heard ye not his Voice
  That ruled the battle dread,
Still echoing from that lofty Shrine,
  Where fleep the patriot Dead?
Charging your Phalanx fair
  In every change to be

The Bulwark of its Native Land,
For Law and Liberty?

You've fought *his* claſſic dome,
  Whoſe eloquence ſublime
Doth make Mount Vernon and its lord
  A theme throughout our Clime.
Your Demoſthenean power
  Made his high ſpirit leap,
Whoſe jewel'd Memory link'd with theirs,
  Unſwerving Fame ſhall keep.

Thanks, Athens! for the cheer
  You on our Braves beſtow'd,
Thanks, ſiſter Rhoda! for the ſmile
  That o'er your features glow'd.
A Mother for her ſons
  Treaſuring all Honor ſhown,
Connecticut with added Pride,
  Thus welcomes back her own.

L. H. S.

Friday Evening, 8 *o'clock, Oct.* 7, 1859.

[From the Hartford Daily Times.]
THE RETURN.

Io Triumphe! The Phalanx forever!
  Unfurl your proud Flag to its own native breezes;
Let the Cynic who ſneered at your early endeavor,
  In this Hour of Fruition ſtill ſneer if he pleaſes;
And let the dull Fogies and mortified Croakers
  Perſiſt in their futile attempts to be witty—
They 're ſubjects themſelves for more jubilant jokers
  Who ſhow the unfortunate Victims no pity.

Io Triumphe! The Phalanx, victorious,
  Returns from its foray in foreign Plantations,
And meets with ſuch Greeting and Welcome, uproarious,
  As thrills ev'ry Soul with delicious ſenſations.

'T is hard to tell which of the two is the proudeſt,
  The Soldierly Troop or the Concourſe ſurrounding;
While excited Outſiders are ſhouting their loudeſt,
  Your own heaving breaſts betray Hearts that are bounding.

Io Triumphe! This, this is the hour
  When ſinewy Strength and tall Intellects mingle;
When the thews and the wits, with a multiplied power,
  Cauſe nerves of admiring Beholders to tingle.
It is Carnival time:—and a rich Gratulation
  Is rained on the heads of the Soldiers, returning,
All wreathed with the bays of a triple Ovation—
  Fit tribute to Genius, Worth, Manhood, and Learning.

Io Triumphe! Bewildered with Bleſſings!—
  And yet all your honors ſo gallantly wearing!
Linked with Man's homage and Woman's careſſings,
  O who would not wiſh in your Paſt to be ſharing.
You 've a grand Picture-gallery for future enjoyment,
  Where Memory gilds ev'ry ſcene as Elyſian,
And furniſhes Dreamers with ſweeteſt employment,
  As Time only ſtrengthens the mental eye's viſion.

Io Triumphe! All ſcathleſs and hearty
  You come, overſhadowed with Laurels and Roſes:
Your Gonfalon, under the ſmiles of Astarte,
  Like Fame's adumbration, in Brightneſs repoſes.
Welcome, then, Soldiers, once more to home duties;
  Welcome, thrice welcome, Battalion all glorious!
Reſplendent with Garlands from large-hearted Beauties,
  Your manifold Trophies proclaim you victorious!

C.

At a regularly called Meeting of the Putnam Phalanx, held at their Armory on the evening of Oct. 11th, the following Reſolutions were unanimouſly adopted, and, by order, were publiſhed in the City Papers the next day, and alſo in Boſton and Providence Papers:

RESOLUTIONS.

WHEREAS, the *Putnam Phalanx*, upon its recent Excurfion abroad, has been received with hearty Welcome and unbounded Hofpitalities; therefore

Refolved, That to the Mayors of the cities of Bofton, Charleftown and Providence, for their eloquent fpeeches of Welcome to the Phalanx, and for the cheering Hofpitalities of their homes—and to thofe of the Municipal Authorities of thefe refpective Cities who participated in our Reception—and the noble Policemen of thefe Cities, who fo effectually guarded our March through their ftreets—this Phalanx tenders its heartieft Thanks.

Refolved, That to the gallant Charleftown City Guard, *Capt.* Boyd, Commander, for its beautiful Efcort, long and heartily continued, and for its bountiful Collation at its Armory, this Phalanx feels under the deepeft obligations—as it alfo does to the fplendid Second Battalion of Bofton, *Major* Rogers, Commander, for its attentive Efcort, and for the free ufe of its Armory. The martial port and bearing of thefe confpicuous Companies, and the attentions fo handfomely beftowed by their Officers, demand, and they receive at our hands our particular Thanks.

Refolved, That we tender our particular Thanks to *Commodore* Hudfon, Commandant of the Navy Yard at Charleftown, for the exceedingly courteous manner in which he received the Phalanx, and for his happy remarks upon the Occafion.

Refolved, That for the courteous and graceful Review upon the Bofton Common, beftowed by the Mayor of Bofton and his affociate authorities, and by the Mayor of Charleftown, and by *Adjutant General* Stone and his noble Staff, our Phalanx feels under grateful obligation.

Refolved, That to the impofing Battalion of Providence Light Infantry, for their Efcort and for the truly magnificent Banquet which they gave to the Phalanx—and for their prefentation of a fragment of the Roger Williams Rock, and for the many kind and eloquent Words of Greeting which they extended, both in public and in private, to our Phalanx, we tender our heartfelt Thanks. They have laid us under a deep and lafting debt of Gratitude, which we fhall be ever willing, but know not how to repay.

Refolved, That we tender our cordial thanks to the *Hon.* EDWARD EVERETT, to *Hon.* RICHARD FROTHINGHAM, Jr., to the *Hon.* GEORGE WASHINGTON WARREN, the Prefident of the Bunker Hill Monument Affociation, and to *Dr.* SEARS, the Prefident of Brown Univerfity, for the highly eloquent and inftructive remarks with which they greeted our Battalion.

Refolved, That to thofe Ladies of Providence who fhowered upon our Battalion the perfumed hofpitality of beautiful bouquets—and to Mifs Mary Putnam Holbrook, of Brooklyn, Conn., who at Moofup Station fo gracefully beftowed upon our Commander a fplendid Wreath—our efpecial thanks are due. Their Prefents were received with lively fatisfaction, and we wifh to the fair Donors, in return, every happinefs.

Refolved, That to E. L. Davenport, Efq., of Bofton, for his polite invitation to the Howard Athenæum—to the Mafons of the fame city for their proffer of civilities to many members of our Corps—to *Private* Ellfworth, of the fame city and alfo of our Battalion, the hofpitality of whofe dwelling was fumptuous and prodigal—to the Commandant of the Providence Light Infantry, *Col.* Brown, and *Commiffary* Davis, for the abounding hofpitality of their manfions—and to all who in any way aided, in any of the Cities we have vifited, to make our ftay agreeable—we tender the affurance of our lively Gratitude.

Refolved, That we thank the Artillery Corps of Bofton and of Pawtucket, and thofe of Warehoufe Point, who honored us with Salutes—as we do alfo the Willimantic Band for its mufic at the Station in their village, which the hafte of the Railroad engineer compelled us, unwillingly, to pafs without a ftop.

Refolved, That our efficient Hofts of the United States Hotel in Bofton, and of the Earl Houfe in Providence, deferve and receive our Thanks for their timely attention to all our wants—as do alfo the Officers and Managers of the Railroads over which we have paffed—and Citizens, generally, wherever they have miniftered to our comfort and pleafure.

Refolved, That to the Hartford Light Guard, *Capt.* Woodhoufe, and the Seymour Light Artillery, *Capt.* Enfworth, of our city, for their cheering efcort upon our arrival home—to our diftinguifhed Fellow-citizen *Gov.* Seymour, for the eloquent words with which he welcomed us—and to our Fellow-citizens generally, who affembled to greet our coming—we tender our heartfelt Acknowledgments. It is indeed a grateful reflection to us all, that the Abfence of the Phalanx was watched with pleafant folicitude, and its Return hailed with proud Satisfaction.

HORACE GOODWIN, *Major Commandant.*

J. M. S<small>EXTON</small>, *Secretary.*

Printed in Dunstable, United Kingdom